The Thinking Tree

Run Win Lead
A Student's Guide to becoming a
Successful Political
Leader

David Lantz & Sarah Janisse Brown

The Thinking Tree, LLC

RUN WIN LEAD
By: David Lantz

With contributions by:

Sarah Janisse Brown
& Georgia Janisse

We use the Dyslexie Font by Christian Boer

FunSchooling.com

Copyright 2025

Reproducible for: Family Use,
By Permission or with Classroom License

TABLE OF CONTENTS

Page 7, Chapter 1: All About You - Creating a 150 Word Introduction of Yourself Specifying your Qualifications.

Page 17, Chapter 2: All About Great Leaders — Complete Biographical Sketches of Davy Crockett and Abraham Lincoln and Identified Qualities that Made Them Great Leaders

Page 37, Chapter 3: All About Volunteering - Analyze Twelve Typical Campaign Volunteer Tasks, Compare & Contrast the Types of Skills

Page 93, Chapter 4: Learning from Experienced Leaders - Focusing on Personal Characteristics and Growth Areas

Page 107, Chapter 5: All About Writing and Giving Speeches — Prepare and Deliver Three Types of Speeches, and Receive Evaluations and Constructive Criticism from an Audience of your Peers

Page 139, Chapter 6: All About the Issues - Complete the Issues Box Assignment, and the Issues Rating Worksheet Assignment

Page 161, Chapter 7: All About Messaging — Campaign Message Exercise, Complete your Campaign Message Box Assignment

Page 175, Chapter 8: All About Building Your Network — Stakeholder Identification Assignment

Page 185, Chapter 9: Your Capstone Project! - Congratulations! You are the Campaign Coordinator for your Congressional Candidate

Page 209, Chapter 10: RUN WIN LEAD - Communicating your vision, developing your voice, leading with honor

INTRODUCTION

Have you noticed that whenever there is an election, there are also a lot of commercials on TV, social media, radio and other places? Then, suddenly, yard signs with the names of people you've never heard of start popping up supporting this or that candidate for some elected position.

Maybe you've never thought about any of this, and you're just frustrated because they distract you from whatever you're interested in.

But maybe, now that you're getting older and thinking about how adults "run the world," you ask yourself: "Do I think that I could do a good job of leading my neighborhood, my town, my state, or even my country?

If the answer is yes, this book will guide you through the process of preparing to run for office, winning an election and leading the people who entrust you with this great task!

We are firm believers that there are three types of people in life: People who make things happen, people who watch things happen, and people who say: "What Happened?"

If you are reading this, you are probably that first type of person — the one that wants to "make things happen." If you are the kind of person who wants to think about helping someone get elected to public office, and maybe even run for office someday in your future — if you're the type of person who says "I want to make things happen for the good of others" - this book is for you.

Ask yourself:
"Do I think that I could do a good job
of leading my neighborhood, my town,
my state, or even my country?"

If the answer is yes, this book will guide you through the process of preparing to run for office, winning an election and leading the people who entrust you with this great task!

CHAPTER ONE
ALL ABOUT YOU

Creating a **150** Word Introduction of Yourself **S**pecifying Your Qualifications.

SOME ASSUMPTIONS WE ARE MAKING ABOUT YOU, THE READER.

As we have put this book together, we've made some assumptions about the typical reader of this material.

PLEASE NOTE: If you don't possess these characteristics, that doesn't mean that you shouldn't read and use this book! It only means that we had to create a picture in our minds of the typical reader so that we could most effectively cover the concepts and ideas we wanted to present.

Also, because of some of the assignments we are going to ask you to do, we assume that you either already know how to do certain things, or can easily teach yourself how to do them.

So, here are our assumptions about you:

- That you are high school through college age.

- That you know how to make reels, videos and post them on YouTube and social media.

- That you can use tools as Google Docs, Canva, Microsoft Word, Excel and Power Point — or can teach yourself how to do basic tasks with these software tools.

- That you can do searches on the internet and use AI for learning.

And that you are a self-starter with an "I can do this" type of personality!

INTRODUCE YOURSELF!

CREATE A 150 WORD INTRODUCTION OF YOURSELF SPECIFYING YOUR QUALIFICATIONS.

We have written "Run Win Lead"
with the following five purposes in mind:

- To help you understand what the various elected offices are for federal, state and local levels of government.
- To help you understand what some of the character qualities of a successful public official are, and the types of experiences that will help you become someone people can trust and vote for.
- To help you understand how campaigns for public office are run.
- To teach you about the types of jobs/tasks which must be performed in running for office, and how you might begin to prepare yourself for a possible run for public office in the future.
- To provide you with resources and examples of how to someday run for public office and start your own political career, if that is something you truly wish to do.
- And finally, even if you never become a political leader, we feel the lessons in this book will help prepare you to become a leader in any effort to which you set your mind.

It doesn't matter where you live in the United States (or even other parts of the world where free and fair elections are held), you can apply the lessons you will learn right where you live.

Having said that, we all have to live **SOMEPLACE**. We (David Lantz and Sarah Brown) live in Indiana. More specifically, we live in what is called the 6th Congressional District in the State of Indiana.
So, examples from the State of Indiana will be used to illustrate the concepts we discuss, but you can search the Internet for similar forms and information where you live.

And, in order to provide some context for our discussion about running for political office, running for Congress in the 6th District of Indiana will be used. We encourage you to apply the same ideas to learn about running for a specific elected office where you live.

Place a colored dot near where you live!

FIRST ASSIGNMENT

You will be writing a short biography of introduction. Here are two examples:

<u>David Lantz</u> (Author of this book)

David is an Adjunct Professor of Economics, Political Science, and Statistics. He was named the **2005** Faculty of the Year by the first graduating class of the Indianapolis Campus of the University of Phoenix. He teaches dual credit political science and economics courses for high school seniors for Ivy Tech Community College of Indiana.

He has worked for such organizations as the Indiana Fiscal Policy Institute and as staff for the Indiana Legislature. He prepared a socio-economic analysis for Dr. Billy Graham's personal use during his **1999** Indianapolis Crusade.

During the early **1990s**, Mr. Lantz served as the State Director of the Indiana Christian Coalition. He has worked on multiple political campaigns, and has trained hundreds of pro-family activists in grassroots political campaigns, and has created an online course titled "**Run Like Lincoln: The Art of Grassroots Politics.**"

His website is: wisejargon.com

Sarah Janisse Brown (Publisher of this book)

Sarah Janisse Brown is the founder of The Thinking Tree, a publishing company that has launched over 300 books for interest-led learning. Her work focuses on helping creative homeschoolers, children with dyslexia, ADHD, and other learning differences thrive through personalized learning. She is the creator of Dyslexia Games, a brain-training therapy used by thousands of families worldwide.

Sarah is a mother of 15 children, including several adopted from Ukraine, and her family life fuels her passion for educational freedom, adoption, and missions. She and her husband, Josh, operate their business from their Indiana homestead.

As former vice president of the Fortville, Indiana Town Council, Sarah led efforts to restore Main Street, bring back festivals, and protect family and property rights. Her leadership blends faith, family, and freedom.

Through writing, public speaking, and international outreach, Sarah inspires families to raise capable, creative children who love learning.

Learn more at funschoolingwithsarah.com

MY BIOGRAPHY OF INTRODUCTION

Look at the short biography of Mrs. Brown and Mr. Lantz (often simply referred to as a "Bio.") Imagine that you want to apply for an unpaid volunteer position with a candidate running for YOUR state's legislature. Write a introduction of yourself, not to exceed **150** words, that will demonstrate your qualifications and cause the candidate to want to interview you about the position.

Start by listing accomplishments, experience, and information about yourself, then write your short bio on separate paper, and copy it to the next page.

Notes:

_____
_____
_____
_____
_____
_____
_____
_____
_____
_____
_____
_____
_____
_____
_____
_____

My Biography:

CHAPTER TWO

ALL ABOUT GREAT LEADERS

Complete Biographical Sketches of Davy Crockett and Abraham Lincoln and Identify Qualities that Made Them Great Leaders.

TO BECOME A LEADER, YOU MUST STUDY LEADERS
Leaders Take Their Followers to The Other Side of the Hill

The Bible says in Proverbs 29:18, "Where there is no vision, the people are unrestrained." Another version reads, "Where there is no vision, the people perish." Regardless of the wording, the message is clear: people thrive under visionary leadership.

If you want to be a successful candidate for political office, you must offer a compelling vision—one that inspires people to follow you into a future brighter than today. One of my favorite quotes about leadership comes from John Quincy Adams, America's sixth President. He said: "If your actions inspire others to dream more, learn more, do more, and become more, you are a leader." This powerful definition emphasizes dreaming big and taking action. It calls you to pursue the knowledge and experience needed to turn vision into reality—and in doing so, become the person God created you to be.

Have you ever had a clear plan in your mind—steps A, B, C, and D—and thought, "This will be easy"? Then reality hits. The process stalls. Why? Because of endless committees and all the people who say, "No, you can't do that because..."

We've all been there—watching promising ideas fall apart. Maybe you've seen a visionary leader say, "Let's go!" only to hand the project off to someone else and move on to the next big idea.

Meanwhile, the person left in charge often lacks the authority, influence, or passion to bring the vision to life. Without the original leader's active support, the project may fail—either because it was never fully embraced or because it carried too many "special interests." What began as a hopeful vision ends up half-hearted and criticized.

So why are some leaders remembered with admiration, while others fade into obscurity?

To give a project a strong start and see it grow into something meaningful, a leader must possess four key attributes—especially in politics, where the goal is to lead people **"to the other side of the hill."**

A Successful Political Leader Must:
- See the Big Picture. This means having a clear vision of "the other side of the hill."
- Communicate the Path. Be able to explain the steps needed to get from here to there in a way others can understand and follow.
- Lead by Example. Don't just direct others—do the work yourself. Then, use your experience to guide others and help them see how their role contributes to the overall vision.
- Build a Vehicle. In this case, that means a political campaign—something people can rally around and use to reach the destination together.

If you ever decide to run for office, you'll need to share your vision clearly—with people who know you and those who don't. You'll need to answer this essential question:

Why should anyone listen to me, or do what I suggest?

_____
_____
_____

Great Leaders Learn From Those Who Have Come Before Them.

Don't think of leadership as a new suit that you can purchase at a store, hang up in your closet at home, and then put it on when you need to do "leadership stuff." Leadership is more about who you are as a person, and the experiences that you have had that shape you into the sort of person who has the qualities of a great leader.

The next few pages will guide your completion of these five assignments:

1. Read biographies of famous people. They don't have to simply be politicians or rulers. I remember reading biographies about Alexander the Great, Davy Crocket, Abraham Lincoln, Marco Polo, Genghis Khan, George Washington, Harriott Tubman and others. Learn about the sorts of struggles they went through that made them into the people we remember them to be.

2. Take a deep dive into a subject you want to know more about. It might be a topic, like entrepreneurship. It might be an historical event, like the Great Depression. Or it might be an historical figure like Herbert Hoover. In order to apply for a college scholarship, I once had to write an essay on entrepreneurship that led me to research all three of the above topics.

3. Learn about the sorts of struggles one or more famous people went through in order to ultimately make a difference.

4. Listen to inspiring speeches. Pick one or more political leaders and find speeches they have given. What motivated them to develop a passion for the topics they spoke on? How did they inspire and motivate others to join them in a cause they truly believed in?

5. Explore other points of view. Use the internet for this research. Find videos on YouTube or other platforms about controversial issues you have an interest in. Get the viewpoint of those who agree with you on the issue you are researching, and also those who disagree with the issue.
Honestly critique both sides of the issue you are investigating.

I. BIOGRAPHIES

Read a biographies of a famous person. They don't have to simply be politicians or rulers. Learn about the sorts of struggles they went through that made them into the person we remember them to be.

I chose to read the biography of _____

Write, draw a picture, and/or create a cartoon
about what you learned:

A STUDY IN LEADERSHIP

DAVY CROCKETT & ABRAHAM LINCOLN

Let's learn from the experiences of Davy Crocket and Abraham Lincoln about the inner fortitude required to run for political office, win elections and lead the people who trusted them.

DAVY CROCKETT

There is no single good answer to how to become a leader, but a great starting point is to expose yourself to other people, other ideas, and other ways of doing things. Here are some ideas on how to get started:

Great Leaders Learn
From Those Who Have Come Before.

In order to do the following assignments about Davy Crockett, you're going to have to do some research. Watch videos or read a book about Davy Crockett.

Here are some links to make it easy:

Davy Crockett had an interesting encounter with a man named Horatio Bunce. The entire story, first published by Harper's Magazine in 1867, can be read here: fee.org/resources/not-your-to-give/

Video dramatic reading: youtube.com/watch?v=LRFaGi2lqrY . History records how Crockett spoke out against Congress giving money to the widow of Stephen Decatur, stating that the Constitution did not give that Congress the power to do that.

Davy Crockett: en.wikipedia.org/wiki/Davy_Crockett see "public career".

BIOGRAPHICAL SKETCH OF DAVY CROCKETT

Below is the beginning of a timetable of Davy Crockett's public career. It contains only a few accomplishments during his political career. Do some research and fill in the blanks to complete the timetable:

a. In 1817, Crockett moved to _____ County, _____ (STATE). He became a _____. Later that year, the state legislature appointed him _____ _____ of the _____.

b. In 1818, Crockett was elected _____ _____ of the 57th Regiment of the _____ Militia.

c. In 1819, resigned from his public offices as _____ _____ of the _____ and from his position from the regiment to focus on running several _____.

d. In 1821, he was elected to the Tennessee _____ of _____. It was during this election that Crockett honed _____ and _____-_____ skills.

e. In 1825, Crockett ran for the U.S. _____ of _____ and lost/won (pick one)? He ran again in _____ and served until _____ when he lost his bid for _____.

f. In _____, Crockett was_____ (successful/unsuccessful) in running for _____ for the _____ time. He _____ (opposed/supported) the Indian resettlement policies of President _____ _____

g. Crockett was _____ for re-election in 1835.
In _____, Crockett journeyed to Texas, where he died in the _____ of the _____. (Source: Britannica Encyclopedia).

ABRAHAM LINCOLN

In order to do the following assignments about Abraham Lincoln, you're going to have to do some research.

Watch videos or read a book about Abraham Lincoln.

Here are some links to make it easy:

Abraham Lincoln:
abrahamlincolnonline.org/lincoln/education/polbrief.htm.bak
and https://en.wikipedia.org/wiki/Abraham_Lincoln

The Act that set the stage for the Civil War was known as the Kansas-Nebraska Act of 1854, Lincoln spoke out against it.

To learn about the act, see youtube.com/watch?v=oWww0Ylf-JE.

To listen to a re-enactment of key parts of Lincoln's speech, see youtu.be/C8A0celaVwY?si=Q-_kmT0rCJMWe78T

Lincoln's House Divided Speech, 1858: youtube.com/watch?v=oWww0Ylf-JE

BIOGRAPHICAL SKETCH OF ABRAHAM LINCOLN

Below is the beginning of a timetable of Abraham Lincoln's public career. It contains only a few accomplishments during his political career. Do some research and fill in the blanks to complete the timetable:

a. In _____, Lincoln declared as a candidate for the _____ (State) _____ of _____. He suspended his campaign to serve as a captain in the _____ Militia during the _____ _____ War. He later _____ (won/lost) that election

b. In _____ Lincoln ran for the _____ (State) _____ of _____ and _____ (won/lost).

c. In _____, as a member of the _____ Party, Lincoln _____ (won/lost) an election to the U.S. _____ of _____. He did _____ (did/did not) run for a second term.

d. From 1849 to 1860, Lincoln served as a _____.

e. During that time, Lincoln argued 175 cases before the _____ State _____ _____ . From 1853 to 1860, one of his largest clients was the _____ _____ _____. His legal reputation gave rise to the nickname "_____ _____".

f. On October 16, 185_, Lincoln delivered his famous _____-_____ Act speech in _____, Illinois. Later that same year, Lincoln was elected to the Illinois _____ of _____, but then changed his mind and decided to run for the _____ _____ _____ instead.

g. In _____ of 1856, Lincoln was considered for _____ _____ at the first _____ National Convention.

h. In June of 185___, Lincoln was chosen as the Republican _____ _____ Candidate. Stephen Douglas was the Democrat _____ _____ Candidate. In those days, the state legislatures chose the US Senator. _____ won the legislative vote.

i. On November 6, _____, Lincoln was elected _____ of the_____. He won re-election in _____, and was assassinated on April 15, _____.

ASSIGNMENT

A. What was the major issue that each man had to face — sometimes taking a position that was not popular even within his own party?

___
___
___

B. What did each man do to prepare himself to argue for his beliefs and prepare to convince others to side with them on their political positions?

___
___
___

C. Abraham Lincoln played a significant role in founding what political party? What political party did a chief political rival of Davy Crocket — Andrew Jackson — help to create?

___
___
___

D. What sort of opposition did each man have to face — in some cases, even from within their own political parties?

___
___
___

E. Describe three things you learned from the experiences of Davy Crocket and Abraham Lincoln about the inner fortitude required to political office, win elections and lead the people who trusted them.

1. _____

2. _____

3. _____

2. DEVELOP YOUR RESEARCH SKILLS

**Great Leaders are Great Learners!
Build your research skills and take a deep dive
into a subject you want to know more about.**

It might be a topic, like entrepreneurship. It might be an historical event, like the Great Depression. Or it might be an historical figure like Herbert Hoover. Prepare to write an essay about the topic.

Topic you chose: _____

Resources you used to learn about this topic:
_____
_____
_____

Make a brief outline of what you learned. Write a short essay on the next pages.

1. (Introduction)
_____
_____

2. First main point
_____
_____

3. Second main point
_____
_____

4. Third main point
_____
_____

5. Conclusion
_____
_____

WRITE YOUR ESSAY

3. COMMON LEADERSHIP STRUGGLES

Learn about the sorts of struggles one or more famous people went through in order to ultimately make a difference.

I chose to research the struggles of: _____

Write, draw a picture, or create a cartoon about what you learned:

4. LISTEN TO INSPIRING SPEECHES

- Pick one or more political leaders and find speeches they have given.

- What motivated them to develop a passion for the topics they spoke on?

- How did they inspire and motivate others to join them in a cause they truly believed in?

_____
_____
_____
_____
_____
_____
_____
_____
_____
_____
_____
_____
_____
_____
_____
_____
_____
_____
_____
_____
_____

DEVELOPING YOUR CAMPAIGN-RELATED SKILL SET

How do you gain the skills to do anything in life? Well, there are two things people generally do. First, they study whatever it is they wish to learn. Certainly, because Abraham Lincoln was a self-taught lawyer, he did a lot of studying about the law, how laws are created, what makes for good laws vs. bad laws, etc. Today, we might call that "book learning."

Davy Crockett spent a lot of time out-of-doors. He observed nature firsthand, and all the things a familiarity with nature teaches us. For Crocket, these included skills like hunting, farming, how to build houses that wouldn't leak when it rained, as well as other skills that were needed by a frontiersman living in the early 1800s. Crockett primarily learned by doing things, just as an apprentice carpenter or bricklayer might learn his trade by working with his father. To a lesser extent, Abraham Lincoln also learned by doing.

A third way of learning is to study people. Both men spent time watching and learning from others. They learned how to persuade others to take their point of view. Thus, another skill set both men developed was the art of communication. This is more than learning how to give a great speech. Good communicators also know how to connect at an emotional level with their listeners. They learn how to impress an important idea on the hearts and minds of their listeners. They learn how to say "I'm just like you," or "I have walked the path you've walked" and not just mean it, but believe it deep down in their souls. All people want to know that the men and women they follow have experienced the same things they have experienced. When men and women develop such emotional bonds, they will not only agree with the leader, they will volunteer their time, talents and treasures to help such a leader succeed in their cause.

Both Crockett and Lincoln knew how to connect with their audiences, and to even learn from their audiences — like Crockett learned from a Tennessee farmer named Horatio Bunce. The story of Mr. Bunce deserves telling here.

"NOT YOURS TO GIVE"

By: Susan Lapin:

As you probably guessed from the lack of boys named Horatio in classrooms today, Mr. Bunce lived in the 1800s. I don't know much of his life story but, like the boy in *The Emperor's New Clothes*, he spoke up and acted when needed. Approached by David Crockett (better known today as Davy Crockett), then running for re-election in Tennessee, Mr. Bunce told the candidate that while he had voted for him in the last election, he would no longer do so. Pressed to explain why, the farmer explained that David Crockett's support for a bill showed that the congressman did not understand the Constitution.

We know of this exchange because David Crockett referenced it in a speech that he later gave in Congress, entitled *"Not Yours to Give"*. It was in many ways an apology to his constituents. It seems that he had supported providing money to families in Washington D.C. who had lost their homes in a devastating fire. As Mr. Bunce explained to him, charity is a function of individuals, not government. Representative Crockett acknowledged his mistake and pledged to not make it again. Mr. Bunce proceeded to campaign for Crockett's re-election.

Source: **Horatio Bunce — American Hero**, February 8, 2024 / Susan's Musings / By Susan Lapin

5. EXPLORE OTHER POINTS OF VIEW

Use the internet for this research. Find videos on YouTube or other platforms about controversial issues you have an interest in.

Get the viewpoint of those who agree with you on the issue you are researching, and also those who disagree with the issue. Honestly critique both sides of the issue you are investigating.

CHAPTER THREE

ALL ABOUT VOLUNTEERING

Analyze Twelve Typical Campaign
Volunteer Tasks,
Compare & Contrast the Types of Skills

VOLUNTEERING

Twelve Tasks Campaign Volunteers Often Do to Help A Candidate Advance a Cause:

In the following pages we provide a brief explanation of what the task is and why it might be done.

For each of these roles or jobs, you will be prompted to do the following:

- Provide an explanation of what the task entails doing.

- Try to provide a real-life example of someone who has done this and the circumstances in which they performed the task.

- List between two and five skills one would need to perform the task.

Here are the twelve tasks, or "jobs" that people often volunteer to do:
(The next section will explain all of these.)

1. Design a campaign mailer.

2. Distribute campaign literature.

3. Gather petition signatures.

4. Make phone calls to potential voters.

5. Research campaign issues and develop "talking points" for the candidate and volunteers to use.

6. Research opposition and negative stories in order to prepare rebuttal talking points that can be used in debates and press briefings.

7. Help organize campaign events.

8. List five event preparation tasks you might do.

9. Write blog posts, text messages, YouTube and TikTok, videos, etc.

10. Help manage the **social media campaign**.

11. Become a volunteer campaign networker.

12. Become a volunteer fund raiser.

DESIGN A CAMPAIGN MAILER

A "campaign mailer" is something that you send to people either through the U.S. postal mail or via email about a candidate or a cause you are supporting.

- Provide an explanation of what the task entails doing.

- Try to provide a real-life example of someone who has done this and the circumstances in which they performed the task.

- List between two and five skills one would need to perform the task.

ILLUSTRATE YOUR LEARNING

Design a campaign mailer:

DISTRIBUTE CAMPAIGN LITERATURE

Campaign literature is designed to be handed out in person, the flyer briefly describes a candidate or cause. It is a shorter version of a campaign mailer that will most likely be thrown away after the person who receives it has looked at it.

- Provide an explanation of what the task entails doing.

- Try to provide a real-life example of someone who has done this and the circumstances in which they performed the task.

- List between two and five skills one would need to perform the task.

ILLUSTRATE YOUR LEARNING

Create a cartoon of you distributing campaign literature:

GATHER PETITION SIGNATURES

Sometimes candidates are required to gather signatures of registered voters in order to qualify for some elective offices such as state governor or president of the United States. There is a specific process which must be followed in order to do so that varies slightly from state to state.

- Provide an explanation of what the task entails doing.

- Try to provide a real-life example of someone who has done this and the circumstances in which they performed the task.

ILLUSTRATE YOUR LEARNING

Draw a picture of you smiling and having fun talking to people about signing the petition!

MAKE PHONE CALLS TO POTENTIAL VOTERS

Get Out The Vote (GOTV) phone calls are made to registered voters in order to get them to turn out to vote on election day/during periods of early voting.

- Provide an explanation of what the task entails doing.

- Try to provide a real-life example of someone who has done this and the circumstances in which they performed the task.

RING. RING.

To make phone calls for a political candidate, you would need:

1. A good speaking voice

2. A positive attitude that one exudes over the phone, even when the response is negative.

3. Attention to detail as you write down contact information and log responses for future follow up when the response is affirmative.

ILLUSTRATE YOUR LEARNING

Write information you should have ready to share about where to vote, hours, the importance of voting, why they should vote for your candidate, and/or questions you may want to ask the potential voter.

RESEARCH CAMPAIGN ISSUES AND DEVELOP "TALKING POINTS"

Talking points are brief, focused statements that outline the key ideas a candidate should communicate when addressing campaign issues. These may include:

- Information about a political opponent's voting record
- Details of an economic or policy proposal
- Memorable slogans or phrases that capture voters' attention
- Core messages on the issues the candidate wants to emphasize

Research the key issues of the campaign and create effective "talking points" for the candidate and volunteers to use:

- Provide an explanation of what the task entails doing.

- Try to provide a real-life example of someone who has done this and the circumstances in which they performed the task.

- List between two and five skills one would need to perform the task.

TALKING POINTS

Write three "talking points" from a past or current campaign. It can be a slogan, information about the candidate or their opponent, information about a specific proposal:

RESEARCH POSITIVE & NEGATIVE STORIES

Track, collect, categorize, and summarize social media posts and news stories related to the campaign. Both the candidate and campaign team need to stay informed about positive coverage that can be shared publicly in support of the campaign.

They also need to be aware of negative or critical content in order to prepare rebuttal talking points for use in debates, interviews, and press briefings.

- Provide a clear explanation of what the task entails doing.

- Give a real-life example of someone who has completed this task, including the situation and outcome.

- List between two and five skills one would need to perform the task.

ILLUSTRATE YOUR LEARNING

Write or draw in each box words or pictures to represent different media sources where you can find information being shared about your candidate.

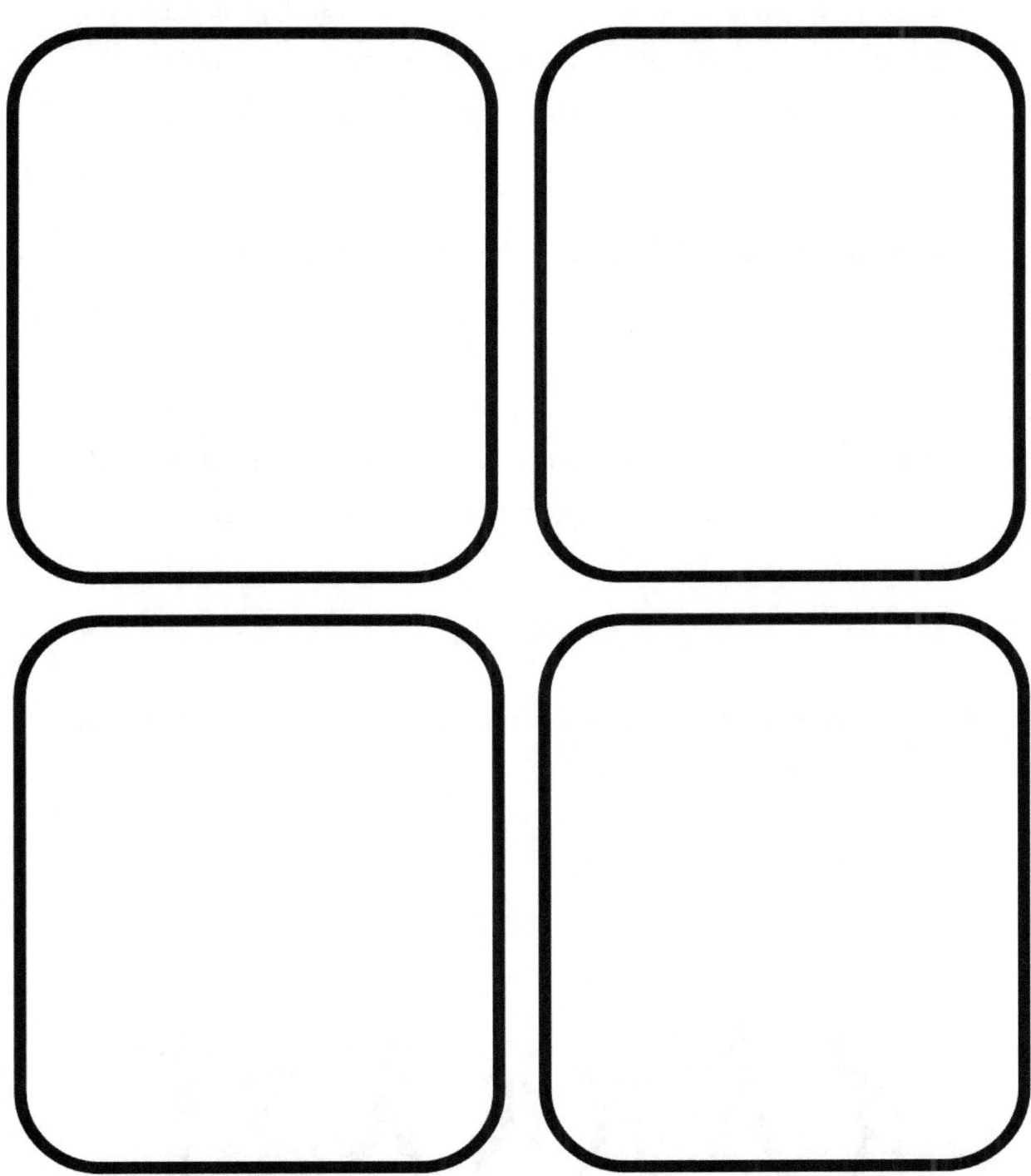

EVENT ORGANIZATION

Event organization is the process of arranging for meetings where people interested in hearing the candidate speak/learn about a campaign topic. Such events can be as small as ten people meeting in someone's home to tens of thousands of people meeting in a football stadium. Many things have to be done in order to make such events a success. **Help organize campaign events.**

- Provide an explanation of what the task entails doing.

- Try to provide a real-life example of someone who has done this and the circumstances in which they performed the task.

- List between two and five skills one would need to perform the task.

ILLUSTRATE YOUR LEARNING

Write or draw what people might be saying or thinking or doing at a planning meeting.

EVENT PREPARATION

Event preparation tasks must be done once an event has been planned and organized. Volunteers are needed to perform many different tasks.

List five event preparation tasks you might do.

1.

2.

3.

4.

5.

- Provide an explanation of what the task entails doing.

- Try to provide a real-life example of someone who has done this and the circumstances in which they performed the task.

- List between two and five skills one would need to perform the task.

ILLUSTRATE YOUR LEARNING

Draw a comic strip of you helping get ready for a big campaign event!

LETTERS TO THE EDITOR

Letters to the Editor is a key way technique campaigns have used to spread their message to the public. The term refers to the time in which almost everyone subscribed to a daily newspaper. Today, the term also applies to communication over the Internet, be it blog posts, text messages, YouTube and Tik Tok videos, etc., that campaigns use to communicate a message to the general public.

Write a "letter to the editor."

- Provide an explanation of what the task entails doing.

- Try to provide a real-life example of someone who has done this and the circumstances in which they performed the task.

- List between two and five skills one would need to perform the task.

Social Media Campaign management is something that all campaigns seeking to share their need to do. The campaign wants to have a consistent message that is being shared across the Internet by all volunteers and paid staff.

Volunteer as a Social Media Ambassador — a person who helps the campaign staff person who manages the social media campaign.

- Provide an explanation of what the task entails doing.

- Try to provide a real-life example of someone who has done this and the circumstances in which they performed the task.

- List between two and five skills one would need to perform the task.

COALITION BUILDING

Coalition Building is a task in which one or more key people meet and network with various groups to help spread positive information about their candidate/campaign issue.

Become a volunteer campaign networker.

- Provide an explanation of what the task entails doing.

- Try to provide a real-life example of someone who has done this and the circumstances in which they performed the task.

- List between two and five skills one would need to perform the task.

Write or draw in each box words or pictures to represent different ways you could meet and network with various groups.
Or write what you might want to say when meeting together.

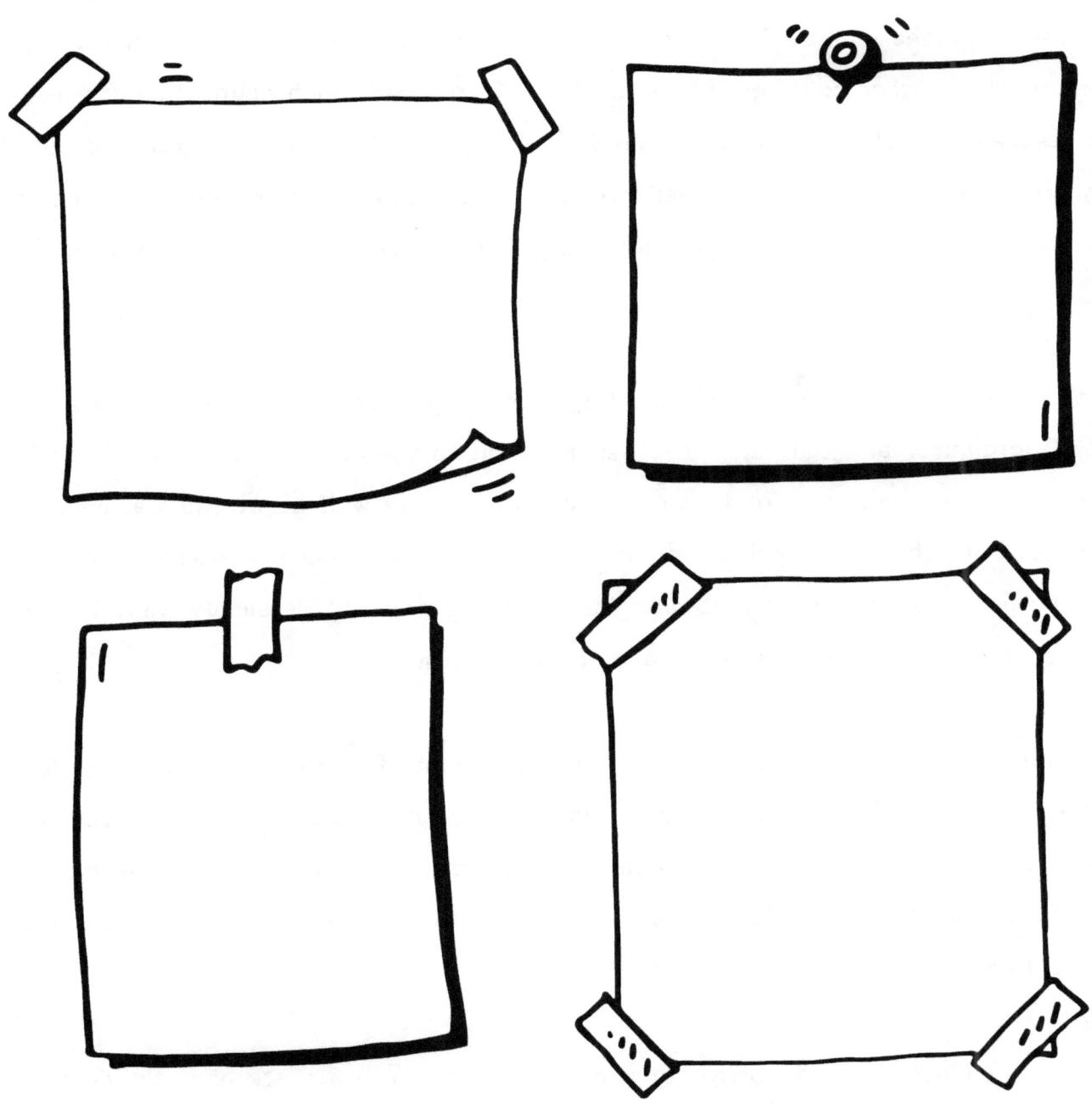

HOW POLITICAL CAMPAIGNS ARE TYPICALLY ORGANIZED

In Chapter One, we asked you to find out about a contested congressional campaign in the state where you live. For illustration purposes, we used the 6th Congressional District of Indiana and looked at the 2024 campaign for that seat.

Here, we want to continue that conversation by looking at how a Congressional campaign might be organized to do many of the tasks you have just researched at the county level. Indiana's sixth Congressional District includes eight entire counties and portions of three other counties, for a total of 11 counties. Each county has its own set of elected officials, its own local news media, and it's own local church and community organizations. Therefore, a well organized Congressional campaign would want to have a County Coordinator to manage many of the tasks you have just learned about.

In putting the following list of positions together, imagine that each county has a County Coordinator and that all the other positions in the county report to him or her. In a real life campaign, some of these positions might very well be at the Campaign Headquarters and be performed for all of the counties in the Congressional District. For our purposes, we don't need to worry about the details — we simply want to think through each of the major jobs that need to be performed.

Even though this example is designed for a Congressional Campaign, the same types of jobs, people skills and campaign coordination are often needed for any candidate, be they someone running for the local school board or the Presidency of the United States. In a small local election a few people often take on multiple roles, and some roles are dropped.

If you are running for a state or national office or helping in a state or national campaign many of these traditional campaign roles will be utilized. In very large campaigns some of these roles are fulfilled by paid staff.

JOB DESCRIPTION OF THE COUNTY COORDINATOR:

Successful politics is the art of a lot of people, each doing a little. In a political campaign, the surest road to defeat is for leaders to try to do everything by themselves. Therefore, a county coordinator must be an individual who is committed to building a team who are in turn committed to an effective **CAMPAIGN** grass roots effort. No manual of "how to" instructions can make someone a good county coordinator. Therefore, in selecting a county coordinator, look for people who have the following qualities:

1. A burning desire to restore our county's greatness based on the campaign's values.

Those who lack an internal source of commitment will eventually fade away. Because the **CAMPAIGN** is an issues driven organization, it is imperative that the county coordinator share the values of the campaign. Therefore, it is critical for the long term success of the grass roots movement that the county coordinator be internally driven and be committed to promoting the campaign's agenda – not his/her own agenda.

2. Political experience.

While political experience can be gained on the job, it is best to find people who already have this experience to fill the county coordinator's position. For example, it is difficult to tell people how to be an effective precinct captain/coordinator if you yourself have never worked in that capacity.

3. Good communication skills, both written and oral.

Most people need someone who can tell them what it is they need to do and how what they are doing fits into the "big picture." People who cannot describe the big picture, how the volunteer's efforts fit into the big picture, and encourage volunteers to perform their role in a positive manner will not be effective county coordinators.

4. Someone who understands how to network with people with persistence and patience.

You get what you inspect. If the county coordinator does not follow up with encouraging words, the effort will fail. Volunteers who respect the county coordinator and share the values of the organization will generally respond to periodic encouragement and follow-up. Understand that you are dealing with volunteers – if you try to "fire" them, they will talk to their friends and contacts and put out the word that you are someone that is difficult to work with. This will ultimately hurt you – and the efforts of the organization.

5. A good delegator and leader by example.

The key to political victory is to find good people, train them, show them how, and turn them lose to replicate the process. The more volunteers you have, the more people doing various jobs, the more successful the campaign will be. It is better to let "technical quality" of something suffer a bit (i.e., letters to the editor, making telephone calls, etc.) by letting people "less able than myself" do the job (somehow, we get the sense that no one can do it as well as we), rather than to limit the work that can be done by doing it all ourselves.

Look over all the skill descriptions needed for county coordinators, and choose four words that stood out to you. Write one of the words at the top of each scroll, then tell why it is an important quality for leaders.

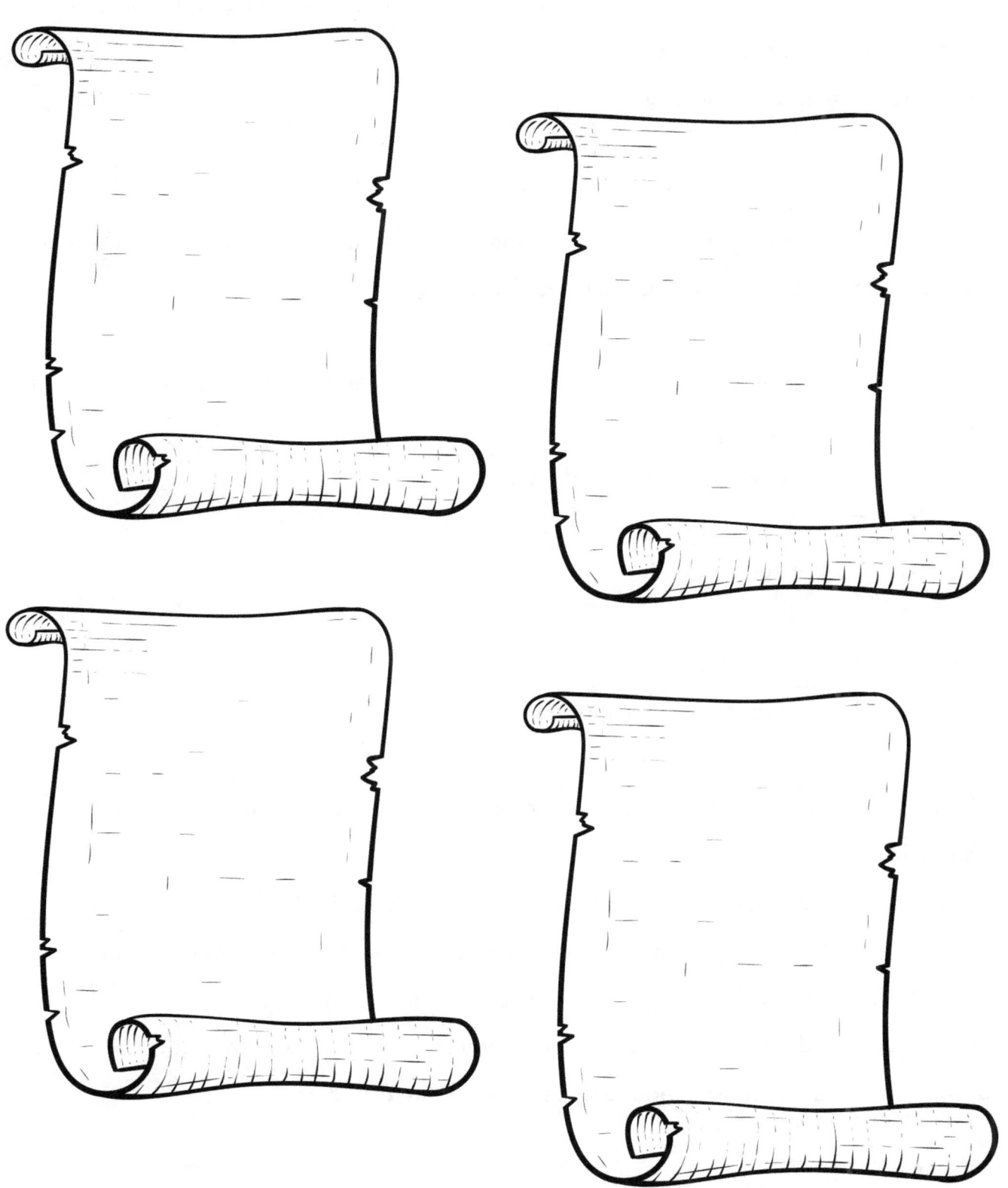

FUNCTIONS OF THE COUNTY COORDINATOR

As the grass roots organization grows and matures, the functions of the county coordinator will change. While you never stop doing any one thing, the job description may be described in three stages:
Infancy, Momentum, and Maturity.

Infancy:

This is a time when you are just building the organization. Duties of the county coordinator at this stage include the following:

Build core group of committee leaders. These committees should include, at a minimum, the following:

    A. Fund raising/event coordinator.
    B. County canvass.
    C. Volunteer recruiter.
    D. Organization liaison.
    E. Precinct captain coordinator.
    F. Communications Committee

- Identify key organizations and individuals with whom to build networking channels.
- Establish initial meetings to organize grass roots effort.
- Obtain key organizing tools, such as a county map, list of organizations, voter registration lists, criss-cross (reverse) phone directory, etc.
- Prepare, schedule and give talks at various groups to explain what the organization is doing and how others can get involved.

Momentum:

During this phase, you have identified a core leadership group which is eager to get going and do things. Duties of the county coordinator at this stage include the following:

- Become the link between your county and the CAMPAIGN headquarters to:
- Coordinate special events/disseminate information.
- Establish committees and work with the executive committee of chairpersons.
- Become the contact person with both political parties and related organizations
- Strengthen ties with various local groups (i.e., Right to Life, Moms for Liberty, National Rifle Association, etc.)
- Become the spokesperson with local media and social media.
- Work with volunteers to train them in the various aspects of precinct organization, speaking to groups, soliciting new volunteers, etc.
- Begin laying plans for what to do during the next election cycle.
- Encourage and give leadership to the volunteers.

Choose one or more of these duties. Share why the duties you identified were of particular importance to you.

_____
_____
_____
_____
_____
_____
_____
_____
_____
_____

Maturity

During this phase of the campaign, you have established a grass roots organization and identified local leadership.

Duties of the county coordinator at this stage include the following:

- Work with the Campaign Chairman to identify what needs to be done during the election.

- Communicate this to the committee leadership and down to the volunteers.

- Identify new leaders to replace those who drop out (i.e., due to illness, death, family crises, moving away, loss of interest, etc. These things will happen, so plan for them.)

- Strengthen campaign ties with local party officials, as well as attempt to influence key local leaders of the county party organization to adopt key talking points of the campaign.

This final stage – the stage of maturity – is the most critical period of any grass roots effort. Heading into the fall election, all **CAMPAIGN** county grass roots organizations should be in this "maturity" stage.

Maturity:

This will be the time of greatest impact, but it will also be the time of greatest danger of splintering and divisiveness. It will be critical for the county coordinator to work to build cohesiveness and dedication to purpose. Remember, people get involved in politics for different reasons - prestige, commitment to a cause, value structure. To keep volunteers doing the political work that must be done - which is often times unglamorous - they must have a sense that the organization is helping them achieve their interests. This will be a balancing act if the goals of the organization are to be achieved.

....

As the fall election approaches, what will be the greatest danger?

What is critical for the county coordinator to do?

What are some reasons that divisions happen?

What can the coordinator do to help volunteers keep working together?

A WORD ABOUT FUNDRAISING

Fundraising is something every campaign must do. Advertising information about the candidate or cause takes money. Typically, such a task is done by an experienced person who has many business and social connections. But there are also many things that go into raising money.

Become a volunteer fundraiser.

Provide an explanation of what the task entails doing.

Try to provide a real-life example of someone who has done this and the circumstances in which they performed the task.

List between two and five skills one would need to perform the task.

Add color to the picture, and then answer her question.

VOLUNTEER RECRUITMENT COMMITTEE

No grass roots organization can function without volunteers. Therefore, the work of the volunteer recruiter/membership committee is vital to the success of this effort. Therefore, the first question is: What will we be asking the volunteers to do? Here are some examples:

Political Work

1. Identify party delegates.
2. Identify precinct committeemen.
3. Identify Poll workers.
4. Identify block captains.
5. Yard sign placement.
6. Identify organization liaisons (i.e., members of churches, community organizations, Republican/Democrat party-related organizations, who share CAMPAIGN's goals and agenda).
7. Write letters to the editor.
8. Conduct County Canvass (see county canvass coordinator job description).

Clerical Work

1. Mailings.
2. Phone calls.
3. Database management.

Communications/Fundraising/Event volunteers.

1. Speakers bureau members.
2. Write letters, PR for special events.
3. Workers at rallies, special events.
4. Event organization.

The volunteer coordinator will want to take advantage of the name acquisition program being conducted by the State Party Headquarters. This program will identify prospective volunteers at the local level who are interested in performing various functions. The volunteer coordinator will want to contact these people and then get them assigned to a particular committee. Furthermore, each of the various committees should be encouraged to recruit their own members, and then report new volunteers to the volunteer recruitment committee to be entered into the database.

(NOTE: HAVING A COMPUTER JUNKIE WORK WITH MAINTENANCE OF YOUR DATABASE IS ESSENTIAL!)

Look over this list of the many jobs that require volunteers to get the work done.

Consider every task listed: from the list of volunteers needed to do political work, to a computer wiz to keep track of everyone, and write down all the positions that interest you the most.

_____
_____
_____
_____
_____
_____
_____
_____
_____
_____

THE JOB OF: VOLUNTEER RECRUITMENT COORDINATOR

In addition to the efforts of the state party, the volunteer coordinator committee will want to hold membership drives. Additional methods of acquiring volunteers include the following:

1. Placing a small ad in the classified section of a suburban weekly newspaper.
2. Watching to see who writes letters to the editor of the local newspaper that take positions in agreement with **CAMPAIGN**.
3. Speaking to church High School youth groups or similar youth organizations.
4. Addressing various civic organizations, including local American Legion posts, pro-family organizations, etc.
5. Toastmasters clubs, which are an excellent source of people who like to speak to people.

Early on, the executive committee should set a goal of the number of volunteers needed, the jobs they will do and the time table for performing the jobs. Communication among the executive committee is vital, and it is up to the County Coordinator to make sure that this communication takes place.

The person who fills this slot should be someone who likes to talk to people and knows a number of people who can do a variety of things. An out going, friendly person is the ideal type. Also, because you will be wanting to reach into different "communities," the committee should have a mix of people from different age groups, social groups, genders, and racial groups.

For example, it is better to send a young woman to speak to a young women's professional group than to send a male retiree. Understand that the audience will most likely respond to a person who shares similar demographic characteristics.

A leader who understands this is an ideal candidate to head up this committee.

THE JOB OF SOCIAL MEDIA MANAGER

In today's campaigns, a strong and strategic social media presence is essential. This may need to be a paid position if a quality volunteer is not available.

Social media is where voters first encounter candidates, where events are promoted, and where trust is built over time. If a candidate or organization fails to show up online with clarity and consistency, they risk appearing out of touch— or being completely overlooked.

Social media isn't just about promotion. It is a powerful organizing and mobilization tool. A well-managed Facebook page or group can serve as a hub for volunteers, supporters, and event updates. Facebook groups are especially effective for coordinating teams, sharing tasks, answering questions, and building a sense of community around the campaign. It becomes a digital town square for your movement.

To use social media effectively, every campaign should have a dedicated manager— someone who understands your message and knows how to represent the candidate's voice online. This person should be skilled in writing clear posts, using photos and video, and engaging with comments respectfully. They should also be able to post consistently and handle criticism without creating conflict.

There are several ways social media supports a successful campaign:

1. Raising awareness of the candidate's platform and values.

2. Promoting events such as fundraisers, rallies, or town halls.

3. Encouraging donations and directing supporters to act.

4. Sharing news and endorsements.

Why a Strong, Updated Social Media Presence is Essential

Your social media is often the first and only impression voters get. It's your handshake, billboard, and town hall in one. If it looks outdated, inconsistent, or amateur, voters assume your campaign is too.

Letting a random volunteer with free time run your socials is risky. You need a strategic communicator—not just someone who knows how to post.

Choosing the Right Social Media Manager

1. Understands Your Message & Voice. Can they write posts that sound like you?

2. Creates Clean, Professional Content Check their past work—do their posts look sharp and read well?

3. Knows Each Platform's Strengths Facebook isn't TikTok. They should know what works where.

4. Handles Feedback & Moves Fast. They need to reply with grace, not panic or silence.

Red Flags—When to Say No

1. Outdated Design Style. If their posts look like a 1990s church flyer, pass.

2. Bad Grammar or Sloppy. Text mistakes reflect poorly on you.

3. Inconsistent or Off-Brand Tone. If they're too ranty, preachy, or goofy—they're not ready.

4. No Personal Engagement. If they don't even share or interact with their own content, why would others?

Bottom line: Your social media speaks louder than your speeches. Make sure it's speaking the right language.

COUNTY CANVASS COMMITTEE

The goal of this organization is to win elections. Winning elections boils down to one basic fact: Whoever gets the most votes wins. Therefore, the key to winning any election is to identify as many of "your" voters and get them to the polls on election day. That is what the county canvass is designed to do.

A county canvass is used to identify registered voters who share your position on the issues. It consists of asking a few questions designed to determine if the voter is one of "our voters," uncommitted, or one of "their voters." It should also help determine whether the person is registered to vote. The county canvass is especially effective in identifying voters who share campaign's position and getting them to vote for pro-family candidates during the primary.

The County Canvass Committee needs to perform the following functions:

- Working with the campaign's headquarters, develop a short script which a telephone canvasser can use when calling and speaking to your party's registered voters over the phone.
- Obtain a list of Your party's registered voters in your county.
- Working with the Volunteer Committee, identify and train volunteers who are willing to make phone calls to identify pro-campaign voters using the approved script.
- Perform voter registration drives at locations and functions (i.e., churches, county fairs, etc.) where people sympathetic to campaign's position may be, and then follow up with a canvass call.
- Circulate petitions which use an issue important to campaign to acquire signatures and build a data base of friendly voters. Follow up with a survey call to see if they need to be registered to vote.

The person who fills this role will need to hold several training sessions in order to train phone volunteers. It is essential that the people making the calls not get into an argument with people over the phone. They must be pleasant and courteous at all times. The phone canvass is not a mechanism with which to change people's minds. Trying to do so on a "cold call" is more likely to antagonize them. Those who do not agree with us we simply do not enter into our data base. Instead, we forget about them and move on. The committee chairman will want to keep in close contact with the phone volunteers, and try to arrange a central location from which to make the calls, if possible.

Write or draw in each different ways to help get people who agree with your candidate to go to the polls and vote.

FUNDRAISING

In any organization, funds must be raised. While the bulk of the money for **CAMPAIGN** will be raised at the state level, local funds will still be needed – and the state organization will need the local organization's help in raising money. At the same time, if events are not held to demonstrate that the organization is "doing something," volunteers lose interest. They need to see that they are part of something bigger than themselves, to see the leaders of the organization thanking them personally for their efforts. The fund raising/event committee works to fill these two roles.

There are a number of ways to raise funds:
1. Garage Sales.
2. Dinners.
3. Golf outings.
4. Small receptions with key donors.
5. Direct mail solicitations.

There are also a number of events which the local organization may wish to help sponsor:
1. Legislative briefings with key legislators.
2. Voter education forums where candidates for local office are invited to come speak about their campaigns.
3. Debates on key issues facing the community.

In each case, these events provide an opportunity to raise money and raise the name recognition and prestige of the organization. The committee, working closely with the county coordinator, will want to stay in close touch with the state **CAMPAIGN** office for maximum effect.

A FEW WORDS ABOUT THE FUNDRAISING/EVENT COORDINATOR:

The individual who fills this position will be networking with some of the more prominent people in the community. Therefore, this individual should be comfortable with working with professional and non-professional people alike. To the extent that some of these community movers and shakers can be invited to be part of this committee, this will increase the effectiveness of the organization. Rotary, Kiwanis and similar professional organizations are good sources of volunteers.

CREATE A CARTOON OF NEIGHBORS TALKING TOGETHER ABOUT A CANDIDATE.

CAMPAIGN COORDINATOR & COMMITTEE

The art of politics is all about building coalitions. Because one should not expect that the members of different - though sympathetic - groups will automatically jump on your band wagon, you will need to have someone in charge of building and maintaining contacts with "friendly" organizations in your community. In this way, you will be able to pass on information from the **CAMPAIGN** to other organizations, and in turn they will be able to supply you with information about which their organization is concerned. If you are unwilling to show an interest in what concerns them, don't expect them to take an active interest in what you are doing.

You will want to build a database of local groups and key contacts in your community. Here is a list of suggestions, there are many more, choose groups that align with your values.

1. Right to Life.
2. Local life chain coordinator.
3. Moms for Liberty.
4. Health Coalition.
5. Tea Party Group.
6. Churches.
7. Republican & Democrat Parties.
9. Business Service Organizations.
10. American Legion, VFW posts.
11. NRA chapters.
12. Patriots.
13. Eagle Forum, Concerned Women for America.
14. John Birch Society.
15. National Federation of Independent Business.

A FEW WORDS ABOUT CHURCHES:

Typically, pastors are reluctant to allow different groups to come in and co-opt their people and their mission. There may or may not be organizations in your state that seek to create these relationships. You'll want to explore this possibility. Generally speaking, it is the lay members of these churches who serve on these issue groups to whom you should address your inquiries. By going through these key church members, you will be more successful in gaining access to the pastors to provide them with the information that you have.

A FEW WORDS ABOUT THE CAMPAIGN COORDINATOR:

This is an area where the County Coordinator will want to be heavily involved, especially when it comes to networking with the local Republican or Democrat Party organization. It will require an individual who understands the value of networking, and has the insight to see that strong coalitions can be built around shared interests in an issue - yet also recognizes that what may be priority issue #1 to one group is priority issue #4 to another group. As political campaigns heat up in your area, you will want to maintain especially close ties, perhaps even getting together with the leaders of several of these groups for general briefings on a regular basis.

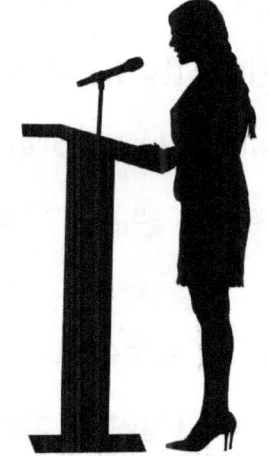

PRECINCT CAPTAIN COORDINATOR & COMMITTEE

The most basic component of any campaign is the precinct. While the County Canvass Committee will be working to identify pro-CAMPAIGN voters and building a data base of these friendly voters, it will be the precinct captain and block captains within his precinct who will be talking to them one-on-one, as neighbors, to get them to the polls and vote. The Precinct Captain Committee will need to do the following:

1. Obtain a list of current Republican/Democrat ward chairmen precinct committeemen. Any precinct which does not have a committeeman, the Precinct Captain Committee (PCC) will want to recruit someone for that position and get the local ward chairman to appoint him/her. The more "friendly" precinct committeemen we have, the easier our task will be on election day.

2. I like to divide each precinct up into three groups: Saints, Sinners and Savables. The "Saints" are precincts which traditionally have a high percentage of your party's voters; the "Sinners" are precincts which traditionally have a large percentage of the other party's voters; the "Savables" are precincts which traditionally have a large percentage of voters who split their tickets between the two parties.

3. Using a census map broken down into census tracts, you will want to first target blocks in those precincts in the "Saints" category, followed by the "Savables" category. If you have enough volunteers, then you will want to target blocks in the "Sinners" category.

BRAINSTORM IDEAS FOR REACHING THE DIFFERING PRECINCTS WITH SOCIAL MEDIA:

There are three groups of people under the oversight of the **PCC**:

1. Precinct Captains. Duties of the precinct captains include:

    a. Check and update voter lists.

    b. Distribute the candidate's campaign literature, door to door, through the block workers.

    c. Identify favorable voters on 3x5 index cards. Obtain name, address, phone number. If they are favorable voters and are not registered, register them to vote.

    d. Recruit volunteer block workers.

    e. Help in voter registration drives by contacting churches, county fairs and other groups to set up registration booths.

    f. Identify "poll checker" volunteers.

2. Block Workers. Duties of block workers include the following:

a. Support the precinct captain and be prompt in reporting to them.

b. Walk your block in the "survey." Determine who is a favorable voter (you may have a list of people identified by the county canvass. Add to this list and verify as you speak to people in person.)

c. Find homeowners who will allow yard signs to be placed on their property.

d. Help register your neighbors.

e. Distribute literature on behalf of your candidate. For example, one might say: "Hi, I'm John Doe, and just live down the street, and I'm a volunteer for (fill in name of candidate). Here is a brochure about him, and I'd like to ask you to vote for him on election day. Can (name of candidate) count on your vote? Thank you!"

f. When a block is completed, contact the precinct captain and let him know.

g. Set up phone banks in the local area to call friendly voters to remind them to vote.

h. As blocks within a precinct are completed and the entire precinct is finished, report to the PCC chairman.

3. Poll Checkers. Duties include the following:

a. Hand out literature.

b. Take the 3x5 index cards used to identify friendly voters. As they come in to vote, check off those who vote and remove that card to another box, leaving only those not yet voting. (Note: Each party appoints a Poll Checker to check off the names of people as they come in to vote. If you sit near the precinct poll checkers, you will hear the voter give his/her name. In that way, you will be able to check off that voter's name from your card file. If you miss any names, you can ask to see the list.)

c. At about 2:00, every "favorable" voter who has not come in should be called and encouraged to come vote. If need be, offer a ride or sitter, etc.

DRAW CARTOONS OF A BLOCK WORKER AND A POLL CHECKER AT WORK

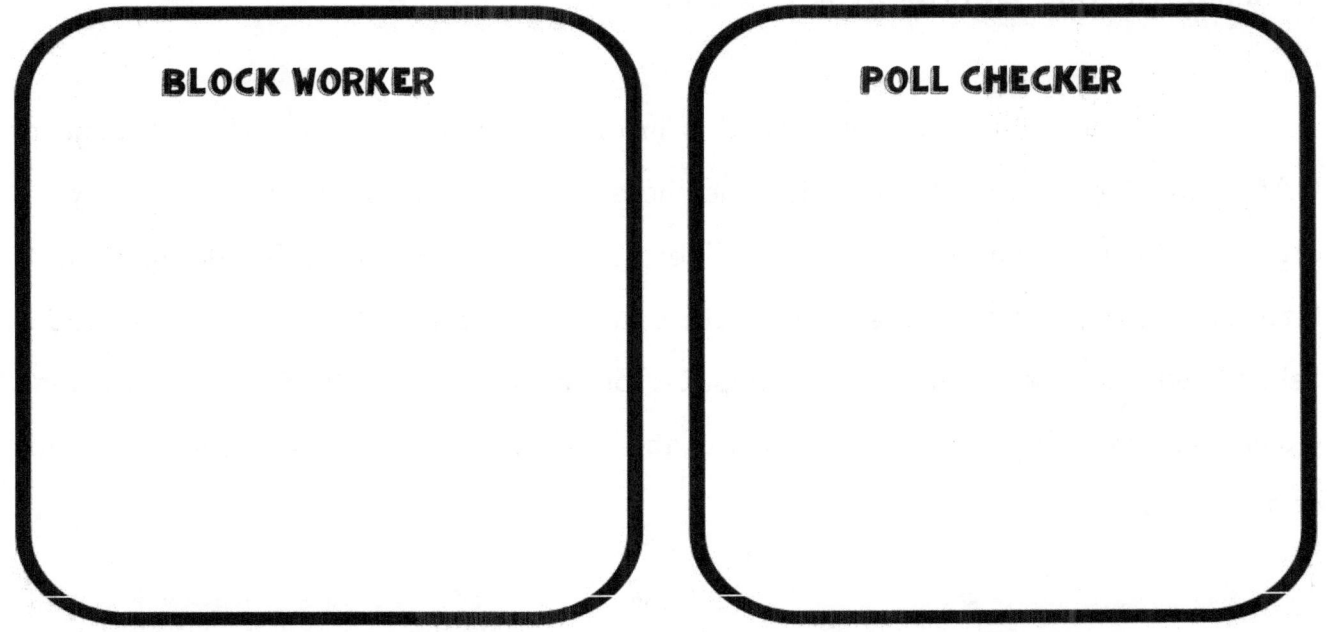

A FEW WORDS ABOUT THE PRECINCT CAPTAIN COORDINATOR:

Clearly, everything else that happens - county canvass, communications, fund raising, organization liaison, volunteer name acquisition - is designed to come together on election day through the work of the **PCC**. Every friendly name identified has to live someplace. Some of these people, even though they volunteer to do other things, may be willing to help in the work of the **PCC**. Because your state's primary or caucus is so important, the walking of the precincts and identifying voters should be done no later than three weeks before the date of the primary/caucus. Furthermore, the precinct captains will need to be advised of when field voter registration ends so that they can be sure to register those who need to be registered in advance of the primary. Finally, it will be important to identify those who will be gone on election day and supply them with absentee ballots.

Personal, one-on-one communication between neighbors - people who know each other - is the best source of advertising. When the election is close the campaign which best accomplishes this will win.

Communications Coordinator & Committee

The communications committee is in charge of making sure the message of **CAMPAIGN** gets out, both to the members of the local **CAMPAIGN** county organization and the general public. There are several vehicles for doing this: Internal organization newsletters, letters to the editor, calling in to local radio talk shows, and being active on computer bulletin boards. The Communications Committee also helps spread the word about **CAMPAIGN** events, such as fund raisers, etc.

While a great deal of information will be provided by the state office (i.e., boiler plate letters to the editor, etc.), it will still be necessary to develop local materials. Here are the duties of the Communications Committee:

1. Develop letters to the editor and find a group of people who will write them and/or submit letter written by others under their name.
2. Develop and maintain a list of media outlets and key reporters/talk show hosts.
3. Help publicize events.
4. Create and publicize social media/video accounts.
5. Write and distribute press releases.
6. Develop and disseminate a local newsletter and/or disseminate one produced at the state level.
7. Develop summaries of positions held by **CAMPAIGN** for dissemination in the community.
8. Develop and promote a speakers bureau.

A Few Words About the Communications Committee Coordinator:

This person should be someone who has previous public relations experience, possibly even newspaper, radio or TV experience. They should know, or develop a relationship with, the media/public relations people in their county. Additionally, they should be familiar with how to use social media and cross platform communications tools. The Communications Committee gets out the message of the campaign leadership – it does not create its own message. Therefore, the Communications Committee Coordinator must be someone who can work with and take direction from the **CAMPAIGN** leadership.

ASSIGNMENT 1 - COMPARE AND CONTRAST THE TWELVE VOLUNTEER TASKS

ASSIGNMENT 1 — Compare and contrast the types of skills and personal characteristics needed to do the volunteer tasks we've been reviewing in this lesson.

Go back through what you wrote about the skills needed to do the various twelve volunteer tasks, as well as what you had to say about the real life individuals you talked about who had done those types of skills. Compare what you wrote to the above description of the various political jobs that need to be done in a Congressional Campaign, as well as the types of people needed to do those jobs. For each of those twelve volunteer tasks, what did you find that was similar in the above job descriptions? Where were there any differences?

_____
_____
_____
_____
_____
_____
_____
_____
_____
_____
_____
_____

**Write up a brief comparison
for as many of the twelve volunteer tasks as you can.**

ASSIGNMENT 2 - VOLUNTEER

Volunteer for a Political Candidate, an Issue Advocacy Group, or a Not-for-Profit organization like a Food Bank, a Homeless Shelter, or your local Church. For this assignment, be willing to do pretty much any task. While it may appear to be mundane and perhaps even repetitive (like stuffing envelopes to do a mailer), any task they might ask you to perform is important to them. Do this task for as long as you like, but for at least two weeks. Then, write a two — three page paper about the experience, in which you describe the following:

- Who / what organization did you volunteer for?

- Why did you choose to volunteer with them?

- What two things did you most hope to learn from the experience?

- What did you do, and what was the "daily routine" of doing whatever it was?

CHAPTER FOUR

LEARNING FROM EXPERIENCED LEADERS

While Focusing on Personal Characteristics and Growth Areas

LEARNING FROM YOUR LOCAL LEADERS

The following pages include some words of advice and encouragement from three friends of mine who have served in local government. Do a little research and find out who is currently serving in a local office in your community. Give them a call or send an email to ask for their best word of advice for an aspiring leader.

Local Leaders to Contact:

Name & Contact Information: _____

Position: _____

Name & Contact Information: _____

Position: _____

Name & Contact Information: _____

Position: _____

Name & Contact Information: _____

Position: _____

MIKE SPEEDY
City Councilman, Indianapolis, Indiana 2004-2010.
Indiana State Representative, 2010-2024,
Congressional Candidate, 2024.

My first experience running for elected public office was for City-County Council in Indianapolis, Marion County, Indiana. It was 2003, and I had volunteered for various campaigns both local, state and federal in the previous ten years up to that point. There was a serious intra-party skirmish. I felt called to serve, and so entered my name to be a leader — and I won!

I attributed my victory to being known as a hard worker for other campaigns. My reputation gave party activists confidence that I'd work hard once elected into the position I was seeking. I was elected as a city councilman in January, 2004, and used my experience to run for state representative in 2010. I won that election, and have served in that position until this year, 2024. As an elected official, I learned that you could disagree on policy positions without making it personal. As a State Representative, I ran for United State representative in 2024. I came in second.

While serving I learned that even when you are unable to offer solutions, you can offer your time listening to constituent's concerns. Ultimately, they are left with a positive impression even when their desired solution was not attainable..

As I consider the advice I would give to a young person considering running for political office for the first time, I would recommend that you volunteer for your political party, or a campaign, and develop the reputation that you are principled, a team player and a hard worker. Even if you don't win, if you are faithfully oriented, then you understand it may not be God's will or timing. Other reasons include it may take more than one effort to establish name identification or build trust with the electorate or for them to get to know you.

AARON NEGANGARD
Circuit Court Judge, Dearborn-Ohio Counties, IN

I was always interested in politics. I remember in 4th grade arguing with fellow students to vote for Ronald Reagan to win the weekly reader poll. He won and I fell in love with politics. My interest in politics is based on my love for this country and its people. People have a disdain for politics but elections have consequences and as such it is critically important to participate.

I was selected to serve out the term of a retiring county councilman in 2004, and served as a prosecutor for three terms and a judge for one term. I was elected Prosecutor in 2006. In 2016, I left that position to work in the State Attorney General's office. In 2022, I ran for the current position of Circuit Court Judge. I have never had an opponent. However, this isn't based on luck but because I had worked very hard helping other people get elected.

The best way to start is by getting to know the people you intend to serve. One of the best ways to get to know people is by helping other good people get elected. I became very successful at helping people win elections. The reputation and network of supporters I built was one of the reasons that when I finally decided to run for office no one wanted to run against me.

The most important thing to remember as an elected official is to always stay humble and remember that you are in that position to serve. The most important advice I can give anyone starting their first campaign is to work harder than your opponent, remember, "eating and sleeping are optional." This was the best advice anyone ever gave me and I have used it ever since to win elections for myself and others at the local, congressional and state level.

ADVICE FROM YOUR LOCAL LEADERS:

NAME: _____

_____
_____
_____
_____
_____
_____
_____
_____
_____
_____

NAME: _____

_____
_____
_____
_____
_____
_____
_____
_____
_____
_____
_____

CHARLES MERCER
Perry Township, Indiana, School Board: 2008-2020

I served on the Perry Township School Board from 2008 to 2020. Although my wife was in the field of education, my vocation had centered around law and government. Our five children grew up in this school system, and so when I was approached by community members to consider running for school board, I said yes. Three reasons motivated my decision: I had just retired from my job at SPRINT and had the time to put into this community. Second, the school board had proved rather dysfunctional in recent years and I thought I could help. Lastly, I was well known in Perry Township, having maintained a strong connection in the community through church and other community functions, and had a reputation of being fair-minded and reasonable.

I'm not sure my experience in running for office was typical. I had a strong group of community members who supported my campaign diligently for months preceding the election. Yet, I, personally, put a lot of effort toward the election. It took money, lots of time speaking to the community, and researching on my part.

If you decide to run for office, understand that to do a good job, you will have to spend time at it. Although running for office took effort, serving as a school board member for the next 12 years required an enormous amount of time with meetings, phone calls, and research. Although I was retired most of my term and had the time to devote to the office, most people are usually not prepared for the time allotment, criticism, and diligence required as a school board member.

INSPIRATION FROM YOUR LOCAL LEADERS:

NAME: _____

_____
_____
_____
_____
_____
_____
_____
_____
_____
_____
_____

NAME: _____

_____
_____
_____
_____
_____
_____
_____
_____
_____
_____
_____

SARAH JANISSE BROWN
Fortville, Indiana, Town Council Vice President: 2009-2012

When I stepped onto the Fortville Town Council as Vice President, I didn't come from a background in politics—I came from my Main Steet front porch, my kitchen table, and my sketchbook. I was a homeschool mom of eight with a newborn in my arms, known for my big ideas and even bigger heart for the community.

But the people of Fortville knew me long before I ever ran for office. It was my husband who said I should run for office. I found it hard to believe I would win!

For a few years before running for office I wrote a column in the local newspaper—sharing stories, insights, and encouragement. It wasn't often political—it was personal. It was about family life, community, creativity, and faith. Those articles helped people get to know me as someone who deeply loved this town and wanted to see it flourish.

On weekends, our home became a safe haven for local teens and tweens. We opened our doors to the youth of Fortville, offering them a warm and welcoming place for wholesome fun, art, music, coffee, conversation, and belonging. It was messy and loud and beautiful. I wanted them to know they mattered—and that their town was a place where they could grow up feeling seen and supported.

My husband, Josh, owned a shop on Main Street, and I was involved in Main Street beautification efforts long before I thought about running for council. I painted vision boards of what our town could become—portraying busy sidewalks, family-owned shops, flower baskets on every lamppost, and art in unexpected places. People began to look at my paintings and say, "Why not?" At the time a majority of the buildings were in disrepair and the sidewalks crumbling.

When I ran for office, I wasn't campaigning on power—I was inviting people into a dream. And I won big — against three other candidates — because the people of Fortville already knew who I was. They had seen my passion, my commitment, and my track record of doing the work.

During my time on the Town Council, I helped bring back festivals to Main Street, cast vision for a revitalized the historic district, and worked to improve the local police force. I made it a priority to listen to the community's concerns and speak up—especially when property rights were at risk. I believed (and still do) in freedom, family, and entrepreneurship, and I often advocated for home-based businesses to thrive in our neighborhoods. My dream was the people of Fortville would love their town, and enjoy the freedom and opportunity offered by the American Dream, without the government getting in the way.

I encouraged people to volunteer, to use what they had—be it time, talent, or tools—and to believe that small acts of care could transform a town. I believed in beauty, low taxes, in freedom, and in giving the people a vision for building and revitalizing the town as a place where families could live, work, and play. In many cases the power-hungry government had been hindering redevelopment and freedom in this small town.

I also attended state gatherings and reached out to state leaders, sharing ideas and helping to inspire similar revitalization efforts in other towns across Indiana.

Looking back, I can say this: I wasn't a typical town council member. I was a mother, a homeschooler, an artist, and a dreamer—but I showed up. I used my voice, my gifts, and my front porch to serve a town I loved. Today the town is a shining example of what the people can do, when they have vison and freedom.

ASSIGNMENT

A. What was the major issue that each local leader had to face — sometimes taking a position that was not popular even within his own party?

_____
_____
_____

B. What did each one do to prepare themselves to argue for their beliefs and prepare to convince others to side with them on their political positions?

_____
_____
_____

C. Did any of the local leaders you talked with play a significant role in any specific initiative?

_____
_____
_____

D. What sort of opposition did each leader have to face — in some cases, even from within their own political parties?

_____
_____
_____

Describe three things you learned from the experiences of your local leaders about the inner fortitude required to run for political office, win the election and lead?

1.

2.

3.

TEN CHARACTER TRAITS YOU NEED TO DEVELOP:

TEN LEADERSHIP SKILLS YOU NEED TO WORK ON:

CHAPTER FIVE

ALL ABOUT WRITING AND GIVING SPEECHES

Prepare and Deliver Three Types of Speeches, and Receive Evaluations and Constructive Criticism from an Audience of Your Peers

DEVELOP YOUR COMMUNICATIONS SKILLS

A key skill anyone who seeks to run for office must develop is their ability to communicate. You will want to improve your listening, writing and speaking skills. This will require practice, and a bit of coaching. One thing you might wish to do is to enter essay writing and speech contests. Whether you win or lose is far less important than the experience you will gain by developing a topic you wish to speak or write about, and then honing your communication skills by competing with others.

Suggested Organizations:

A. **Optimist Club** Here is the application for their **2023/24** speech contest: optimist.org/documents/2024/programs/23-24_Oratorical_Application.pdf

B. **Toastmasters International**: This organization helps you learn how to give speeches. They have a program for teenagers: www.toastmasters.org/magazine/articles/teaching-presentation-skills-to-kids# Find a local Toastmasters Club in your area to see about joining (or developing) such a club for adolescents and teens.

C. **National Right to Life Essay Contest**: nrlc.org/essaycontest. Right To Life also sponsors a speech contest: nrlc.org/oratorycontest

D. **NCFCA Christian Speech & Debate.** This organization works with youth in Christian home school communities to sharpen their speech and debate skills. Many states, including Indiana, have organized speech and debate contests you can learn about and participate in: ncfca.org

E. **Future Farmers of America** sponsors a speech contest on agricultural topics: ffa.org/participate/prepared-public-speaking

F. **Knights of Columbus** sponsors essay contests for Catholic high school students. To learn more, visit kofc.org/en/what-we-do/faith-in-action-programs/community/catholic-essay-contest.html

There are probably many other local organizations you can participate in. Do your own research to find one that you are interested in where you live. Some even offer scholarship opportunities depending on how well an entrant does in their respective competitions.

The Five Questions You Must Answer When Preparing to Give a Speech:

There are many videos about giving speeches on Youtube. Rather than spend time about how to give a speech in this book, it would be more beneficial for you to go out and research the topic of giving speeches on your own.

Instead, we suggest that you spend your time working on three speeches that are the type someone running for office might give. I (David Lantz) spent 15 years in Toastmasters International, so the ideas for how to develop these three speeches comes from my experience with that organization.

These speeches are:

1. **The Introductory Speech** — a speech in which you introduce yourself to an audience that knows little or nothing about you.
2. **The Informative Speech** — a speech where you inform an audience about a topic they may know little about, but which you are well informed.
3. **The Persuasive Speech** — a speech where you seek to persuade an audience to adopt/agree with a viewpoint you hold.

As you work to develop these three types of speeches, pay attention to the way speeches are developed and organized and delivered for the greatest effect. For each of these speeches, rehearse them so that you can deliver them without notes. Find a group of family or friends (three or more) who will listen to you and give you constructive feedback.

FIVE QUESTIONS TO ASK YOURSELF BEFORE BEGINNING TO PREPARE YOUR SPEECH.

1. Who is my audience, and why are they listening to me?

2. When I am done giving this speech, what goals do I hope to have accomplished (try to focus on three specific goals)?

3. What are the key ideas I want to communicate to **THIS** audience?

4. Does the audience view me as someone who is a credible speaker on this topic, or as someone who is a "pretender" and are therefore likely to treat my presence and the words I have to say with skepticism?

5. What examples, stories, or facts do I need to present to **THIS** audience to gain their trust and support given the way they view me as a credible speaker on this topic (see point #4)?

COPY THESE FIVE QUESTIONS THAT YOU NEED TO ASK YOURSELF BEFORE BEGINNING TO PREPARE YOUR SPEECH.

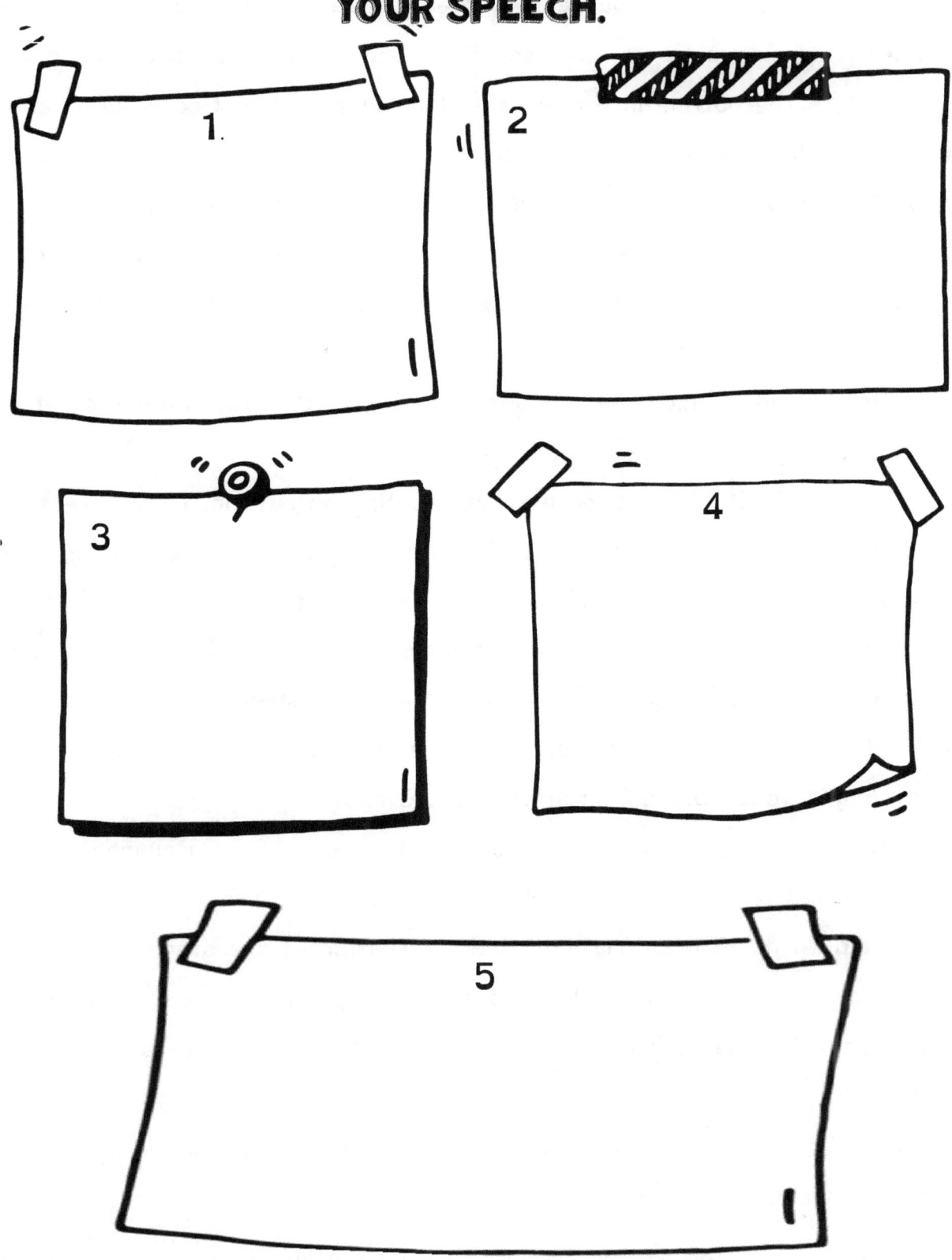

As you go about preparing your speeches, start out by constructing an outline. Once you have the rough outline, try giving a speech to yourself in the mirror. Does it flow? Do you need to re-organize the order of topics in the outline? Did you realize you left something out? Once you have refined your outline, turn the outline into a written document that you could print as a blog post on the Internet if you wished to. Keep in mind that your goal is to be able to **COMMUNICATE** your ideas. Doing so orally is only one way. Doing so in written form is also key. A third way to communicate is via video — for example, creating a Youtube presentation of your speech illustrated with visual effects.

Several years ago, I self-published a book titled *The Unraveling of We The People* wisejargon.com/leadership/the-unraveling

I began writing the book by first creating an outline. I then created individual blog posts as I worked to fit everything into a book (here is a link to some of those blog posts wisejargon.com/category/the-unraveling). Once the book was published, I gave various speeches on the book. One such speech was video recorded. I broke up the video recording into several short videos. The first video in which I begin my speech is this one titled "**Is America Unraveling?**" youtube.com/watch?v=ovj05DQnm04

The video clip is less than three minutes long. Take a moment to watch the video, and then answer the following three questions:

1. What did I do to grab the audience's attention at the start of the speech?
2. How did I build rapport with the audience — by that I mean, how did I connect with the audience to demonstrate that I shared a heartfelt concern they had?
3. What is the problem that I identify — a problem that I am going to address as the speech unfolds?

Seriously. Stop reading now and watch the video. If possible, watch it with a small group of others, and then discuss the above three questions.

Answer these questions about the speech "Is America Unraveling?"

1. What did I do to grab the audience's attention at the start of the speech?
___
___
___
___
___

2. How did I build rapport with the audience — by that I mean, how did I connect with the audience to demonstrate that I shared a heartfelt concern they had?
___
___
___
___
___

3. What is the problem that I identify — a problem that I am going to address as the speech unfolds?
___
___
___
___
___

THREE TYPES OF SPEECHES TO DEVELOP

As we said, the best way to learn how to give a speech is to actually give a speech. Let's work through the process of giving the three types of speeches we mentioned earlier: **The Introductory Speech, the Informative Speech, and the Persuasive Speech.**

THE INTRODUCTORY SPEECH

At some point in your political career, people will want to learn about you. Who are you? What makes you tick? Imagine you have just joined an organization, and they've asked you to say a few words to tell people who you are. Here are some tips:

- **You don't want to tell everything about your life,** so pick some sort of general theme about yourself that you can provide three or four short stories about. Perhaps it is an interest that you have and how that interest has grown to be the thing you wish to do as a career or avocation.

- Tied to this **over-arching theme**, talk about how it has led you to develop goals for yourself. How you have achieved some goals in the past, and how doing so opened new doors/new opportunities for you.

- Often times, people gravitate to groups of three, so consider numbering your **stories/examples, limiting them to just three.**

- Create an interesting opening. If I were to start an introductory speech about myself, it might go like this:

I was just six years old, and my father was very angry. He was so angry, he stormed out of the room. I asked my mother what I had done wrong. She put down her newspaper, smiled at me, and said: "David, you just beat him in a game of chess. And your father hates to lose at anything." That day began my journey to become the captain of my high school and college chess teams, and to love how the thought process of thinking multiple moves ahead in a simple game could be applied to the study of economics and politics.

Reflecting back on my life, the study of ideas, and how they can be combined to produce new ways of doing things sprang from my love of the game of chess. It's a game in which the minds of two opponents are locked in mortal combat across a board with sixty-four squares. I've applied that competitive spirit in many different ways throughout my life.

- After introducing yourself, provide three main points, and think of a simple but effective method of transitioning to the next point. Think of each main point as a steppingstone, which allows you to advance from one thought to the next, helping your audience to see the connection in a natural progression as simple as **1. 2. 3.**

- End with a conclusion that ties the talk together. Leave them wondering what the future has in store. Invite your listeners to follow you and share in the journey to see where the story takes you next.

- Keep the speech to between **5** and **7** minutes.

THE INFORMATIONAL SPEECH

There are no doubt many topics you might speak about. There might be more than one viewpoint on your topic — some you agree with, some you disagree with. For this speech, focus on giving the facts — the background — to the topic. Provide information to inform. We'll get to persuading in the next speech. The key for this speech is to choose a topic that is meaningful to you. Your goal should be to get people to care about a topic that you are passionate about. If you don't care about it, don't expect others to care about it either.

Think about composing your speech. In the **Introductory Speech**, I suggested

that you talk about your life as a series of connected stories built around a common theme (in my example, learning to apply the thought process of playing chess to other events in my life). For this speech, the structure of your story should consist of three parts: An introduction, the main body (with, you guessed it, **THREE** main points connected with transitions), and a conclusion. As with the Introductory Speech, practice it so that you can deliver the speech without notes. Plan on the speech being 5 — 7 minutes in length.

1. Introduction

Your **introduction** is intended to grab audience members' attention while introducing your topic. Did you watch the video clip I shared earlier in **"Is America Unraveling?"** I talked about a question my daughter asked me when she was a Junior in high school and used that story to connect to the purpose of my talk.

2. Body

Next, move to the **body** of the speech. Each section should pertain to a single idea with clear transitions to the next section. This process of choosing transitions can be challenging. There are basically five ways you might organize your material, depending on the topic you have chosen:

1) **Chronologically** organized speeches follow a sequence of events.

2) **Topically** organized speeches divide the topic into sections that explain major concepts which then narrow down to specific examples/subtopics.

3) **Spatially** organized speeches relate to geographically related subjects, such as the Battle of Gettysburg and the geographic landmarks that played a role in each phase of the battle.

4) **Causally** organized speeches link a cause to an effect, or an effect to its cause.

5) **Comparatively** organized speeches describe two or more things which compares them by examining their similarities and differences.

Your choice of **HOW** you present your material should be dictated by your answers to the following three questions:

a. What is the most important thing I want to say?

b. Why does what I say matter to the audience?

c. What do I want people to do/think/believe as a consequence of what I say?

The final section of your speech is the **conclusion**. A good practice to follow when giving a speech is to do the following: Tell them what you're going to tell them. Tell them. Tell them what you told them. In other words, use the example you gave in the introduction of your speech. Mention it again in your conclusion, and how your speech has served to explain your primary message in the body of the speech. This doesn't mean you should repeat yourself, but that you should have one consistent message that the listener will remember. Use the introduction to build interest and curiosity about your primary message. The main body will lead listeners to greater understanding, and in the conclusion summarize the key points in a way that will leave a lasting impression.

> Think of your interests, topics you believe are important for others to understand, or what you enjoy telling people about, and list them here:

Choose one of the topics you listed on the previous page and answer these three questions:

My topic:

_____

_____
_____
_____
_____
_____

Why does what I say matter to the audience?

_____
_____
_____
_____
_____

What do I want people to do/think/believe as a consequence of what I say?

_____
_____
_____
_____
_____
_____
_____
_____

THE PERSUASIVE SPEECH

The Persuasive Speech is similar in structure to the informational speech. The key difference is that you wish to persuade the audience to adopt your point of view/conclusion on a topic. Think of any TV show or movie where lawyers have to argue a case before a jury. Evidence must be presented, motive must be established, and the jury must be led to conclude beyond a reasonable doubt that what you are saying is true, that your solution is in their best interests, and that you have no ulterior motive for presenting the evidence to them.

As with the previous speeches, rehearse it so that you can deliver the speech without notes. Plan on the speech being 5 – 7 minutes in length. You will want to create an attention grabbing opening, construct the body of your speech, and provide a strong conclusion which, in this case, calls on your audience to take some sort of action.

HERE ARE SOME TIPS:

1. Research your audience.

Where do they stand on the topic you are going to present. It may be that they share some or all of your concerns, but may already have a different solution in mind. It may be that they believe certain things about your topic, but their understanding is based on faulty information. For these and other reasons, your task may be to change the audience members' opinions or persuade them to develop the same opinion you have.

2. Know Your Audience

There are five different types of audiences you are likely to speak to.

The Agreeable Audience: In politics, this is known as your political "base." They already agree with your opinion or viewpoint. Your goal is to strengthen and reinforce this agreement to motivate them to get the vote out for you, volunteer for you, and financially support your campaign.

The Apathetic Audience: While this group may be interested in your proposals/values, a key factor for them is the question "what's in it for me?" For this type of audience, a key objective should be to convince them that the issue has a direct effect on their lives.

The Hostile Audience: Such an audience is likely hostile to you for one of three reasons: First, they know your position and are strongly against it. Second, they have a material interest in opposing whatever it is you say. Third, they have been told half truths or even outright lies about you/your message by your opponents. You must find out why they oppose you before they hear a word of your speech, and frame your remarks to respond to that key barrier. Only then can you hope to gain their attention to listen to what you have to say.

The Uninformed Audience: Your listeners may be completely unfamiliar with you or your subject. You must first establish your credibility, and then provide evidence they will accept so that you can educate them about your campaign or issue.

The Varied Audience: This type of audience contains a combination of audience members. You must include content that informs, convinces audience members of your subject's importance, demonstrates the merits of your viewpoint, and expresses why they should reconsider their own views.

3. Inspire your audience. This is best accomplished when you can speak about an issue in such a way that you reinforce their existing ideas and beliefs. If they do not already have some basis of agreement with you, you will be unlikely to move them to act as you hope in a single speech. The goal is to inspire excitement in your audience about your topic or reinforce their existing ideas and beliefs.

There are three modes of persuasion: **Morality, logic,** and **emotion**. Think through what it is you are wishing to persuade the audience of, and use the approach that is best suited to the circumstances.

   a. **Morality** is about credibility as a speaker on this topic. An audience needs to accept you as knowledgeable, trustworthy and empathetic to their circumstances before considering changing their opinions.

Look up the definition of these words:

Morality:

Knowledgeable:

Trustworthy:

Empathetic:

b. **Logic** is a part of every persuasive speech. Does what you have to say pass "the smell test?" An "If, Then" statement would be something like this: "IF the only way you, as a poor woman, can get welfare benefits, is to make sure there is no 'man in the house,' THEN what must you do about the deadbeat husband you are married to?" The logical answer is: Get divorced or lie about there being "a man in the house." This was a key argument put forward for why welfare benefits were reformed in 1997, as it was discovered that the "man in the house rule" of a federal welfare program called Aid to Families with Dependent Children" actually led to an increase in divorce and out of wedlock childbirth. If you can lead your audience to see the logical conclusion of an idea, you can win their agreement, as Professor Charles Murray did when he discussed the above issue in his book: *Losing Ground: American Social Policy, 1950-1980*.

Look up the definition of the word logic:_____

c. **Emotion** can contribute a powerful influence when used in the right circumstances. Evoking emotions such as happiness or empathy in listeners and relating these to your topic is a powerful tool. A key rhetorical tool to use when generating an emotional response is to lead the audience to join you in repeating a phrase that emphasizes the point you are making.

Define these words:

Emotion: _____

Happiness: _____

Empathy:_____

Rhetorical device:_____

AN EXAMPLE OF A SPEECH TO ANALYZE

On March 23, 2024, I gave a speech before the Indiana Republican Assembly (INRA) on behalf of Mrs. Jamie Reitenour, who was running for Governor of Indiana. I knew going in that the audience generally shared the values of both myself and my candidate, Jamie Reitenour. I also knew it was a varied audience, as part of the crowd included supporters of other candidates. My job was to introduce Mrs. Reitenour and counter the argument that she had no "political" experience. I had to talk about the issues she supported and emphasize her credibility on these issues. I also had to establish my own credibility as to why I was qualified to speak on her behalf.

In giving that speech, I used a rhetorical device to create emotional rapport with the audience so that they would be moved to vote for my candidate. You see, later that day, a straw poll was taken on the gubernatorial candidates the membership of the INRA might wish to support. My candidate, Mrs. Jamie Reitenour, won 76% of the vote cast. As an example of a political persuasive speech, I offer you the following; "The speech that won Jamie Reitenour 76% of the INRA straw-poll"

Watch my speech: www.youtube.com/watch?v=h9aXCVX0x34

As you watch this speech, answer the following questions:

1. Notice in my introduction about myself, I connected my experience to things I had done that express my faith in Jesus Christ. How did I know that this audience would appreciate this? Go to the national organization's website at nationalrepublicanassemblies.com/what-we-believe to find out.

2. Mrs. Jamie Reitenour had been criticized for not ever having been elected to a political office in the past — that she had no political experience? In the informational part of my speech, how did I address this criticism?

3. In the persuasive part of my speech, I used a rhetorical technique to involve the crowd emotionally in what I had to say in order to build support for Mrs. Reitenour in the Straw Poll Vote that followed. What was that technique? (Noice that Governor Ann Richards uses a version of this technique in her 1988 Democrat Convention speech, in which she repeated the phrase "he can't help himself. He was born with a silver foot in his mouth". And here is a clip from Jean Kirkpatrick's 1984 Republican Convention speech about the "Blame America First Crowd.")

ASSIGNMENT: Imagine a group of people to whom you would like to speak. Describe the audience. What are their interests? Why might they come listen to you? Invite them to come hear you give three, five-to-seven-minute talks. These talks (taken from the Toastmasters International Level One speech training series) are:

1. The Introductory Speech— where you tell about yourself.

2. The Informative Speech — where you pick a topic with which are knowledgeable and explain it to others whom you believe would be interested in learning about it. This does not have to be a political topic and would actually be best if it were not a political topic.

3. The Persuasive Speech — where you pick a topic you care about and want to persuade the audience to not only agree with your position but are motivated to take action to do something about it.

Create a document that listeners can use to evaluate each of your talks.

- Provide room to provide constructive criticism/earned praise.
- This Evaluation form should look something like the following.

	Excellent	Good	Ok	Needs Work
Pace: Did the speaker speak at a good pace and use pauses for good effect.				
Enunciation: The speakers were clear, not slurred. Diction was clear and distinct.				
Fillers: The speaker did not use "filler" words like "Um, you know, like, etc."				
Eye Contact: The speaker established good eye contact with multiple audience members.				
Transitions: As the speaker moved from point to point, the speech flowed well and the transitions were logical.				
Overall Effect: I was moved to agree with the speaker and to follow his/her recommendations.				

INFORMATION BLOCK

In order to help you develop these three speeches, you can find many resources on the internet. Toastmasters International has a wealth of information. Their organization is devoted to helping members become better listeners, thinkers and speakers. As a member of Toastmasters International for fifteen years, I participated in and won many speech contests. The following documents and videos will get you started on preparing the three speeches we've suggested that you do:

Giving an Icebreaker Speech:
youtube.com/watch?v=4dG2O3xDrlI and toastmasterscdn.azureedge.net/medias/files/pathways/2021-updates/8101-ice-breaker.pdf

Giving a Persuasive Speech:

youtube.com/watch?v=jnfoFN7TBhw

Giving an Inspirational Speech:

toastmasters-lightning.org/wp-content/uploads/2021/02/8305-Inspire-Your-Audience.pdf

youtube.com/watch?v=7bVSOJL57F8

Speaking to inform:

toastmasterscdn.azureedge.net/medias/files/pathways/2021-updates/8103-writing-a-speech-with-purpose.pdf

Take notes as you watch, listen to or read the information linked in the information block.

ICEBREAKER SPEECH

_____
_____
_____
_____
_____
_____
_____
_____
_____
_____
_____
_____

PERSUASIVE SPEECH

_____
_____
_____
_____
_____
_____
_____
_____
_____
_____
_____
_____

INSPIRATIONAL SPEECH

INFORMATIVE SPEECH

DRAW A COMIC STRIP OF YOU PREPARING AND GIVING A SPEECH.

PERSUASIVE SPEECH

Create an outline of your persuasive speech

Use the form on the next page to record
the results from your listeners evaluations

	Excellent	Good	Ok	Needs Work
Pace: Did the speaker speak at a good pace and use pauses for good effect.				
Enunciation: The speakers were clear, not slurred. Diction was clear and distinct.				
Fillers: The speaker did not use "filler" words like "Um, you know, like, etc."				
Eye Contact: The speaker established good eye contact with multiple audience members.				
Transitions: As the speaker moved from point to point, the speech flowed well and the transitions were logical.				
Overall Effect: I was moved to agree with the speaker and to follow his/her recommendations.				

INSPIRATIONAL SPEECH

Create an outline of your inspirational speech

_____
_____
_____
_____
_____
_____
_____
_____
_____
_____
_____
_____
_____
_____
_____
_____
_____
_____
_____
_____

Use the form on the next page to record the results from your listeners evaluations

	Excellent	Good	Ok	Needs Work
Pace: Did the speaker speak at a good pace and use pauses for good effect.				
Enunciation: The speakers were clear, not slurred. Diction was clear and distinct.				
Fillers: The speaker did not use "filler" words like "Um, you know, like, etc."				
Eye Contact: The speaker established good eye contact with multiple audience members.				
Transitions: As the speaker moved from point to point, the speech flowed well and the transitions were logical.				
Overall Effect: I was moved to agree with the speaker and to follow his/her recommendations.				

INFORMATIONAL SPEECH

Create an outline of your informational speech

_____
_____
_____
_____
_____
_____
_____
_____
_____
_____
_____
_____
_____
_____
_____
_____
_____
_____
_____

Use the form on the next page to record the results from your listeners evaluations

	Excellent	Good	Ok	Needs Work
Pace: Did the speaker speak at a good pace and use pauses for good effect.				
Enunciation: The speakers were clear, not slurred. Diction was clear and distinct.				
Fillers: The speaker did not use "filler" words like "Um, you know, like, etc."				
Eye Contact: The speaker established good eye contact with multiple audience members.				
Transitions: As the speaker moved from point to point, the speech flowed well and the transitions were logical.				
Overall Effect: I was moved to agree with the speaker and to follow his/her recommendations.				

CHAPTER SIX

ALL ABOUT THE ISSUES

Complete the Issues Box Assignment, and the Issues Rating Worksheet Assignment

IDENTIFYING WINNING CAMPAIGN ISSUES

Campaign issues come and go. What is a major concern in one election cycle may garner little attention in another time period. As a candidate for office, three things are important in choosing issues to run on. **First**, what issues are important to you as a candidate for office? You can't be a credible spokesperson on an issue if you care nothing ABOUT that issue. **Second**, what issues are important to the voters? You may care a great deal about something, but unless the voters also care a great deal about that issue or a related issue, you will be like a car on an icy road: You will spin your wheels but gain very little traction.

The **third** factor that determines whether you should incorporate an issue into your campaign is whether the public considers you to be a credible and trusted speaker on that issue. For example, an economist who describes his ideas about promoting jobs in depressed economic areas might well be considered as a credible spokesperson on the topic. But, if a well-spoken individual has lived in an economically depressed area where those ideas have been tried — and shown not to work — the second individual's personal experience may be viewed as superior to the economist's academic experience. This would be especially true if the economist came from a high income family that had never lived in an economically depressed area.

It won't always be immediately obvious why one candidate is better "qualified" to speak on an issue than another person. It is a bit in the "eye of the beholder." However, surveys of voters and informal discussions can help to find out the answer to this and other issue related questions. Thus, if you're running for office, there are a few questions you need to answer.

What are some issues that you are interested in? What issues are important to you?

CREATING A PUBLIC PLATFORM

Learning from the 2024 Presidential Campaign

A good place to start to discover what the issues are is to consult a political party's issues platform. Every four years, the major political parties gather at both the state and national level to hammer out a set of issues they want all of their party's candidates to support.

REPUBLICAN PARTY STATEMENT:

"To make clear our commitment, we offer to the American people the 2024 GOP Platform to Make America Great Again! It is a forward-looking Agenda that begins with the following twenty promises that we will accomplish very quickly when we win the White House and Republican Majorities in the House and Senate."

REPUBLICAN PARTY 2024 PRESIDENTIAL PLATFORM

1. Seal the border and stop the migrant invasion.

2. Carry out the largest deportation operation in American history.

3. End inflation and make America affordable again.

4. Make America the dominant energy producer in the world—by far.

5. Stop outsourcing and turn the United States into a manufacturing superpower.

6. Large tax cuts for workers, and no tax on tips.
Defend our Constitution, our Bill of Rights, and our fundamental freedoms—including freedom of speech, freedom of religion, and the right to keep and bear arms.

7. Prevent World War III, restore peace in Europe and the Middle East, and build a great iron dome missile defense shield over the entire country—all made in America.

8. End the weaponization of government against the American people.

9. Stop the migrant crime epidemic, demolish the foreign drug cartels, crush gang violence, and lock up violent offenders.

10 Rebuild our cities—including Washington, D.C.—making them safe, clean, and beautiful again.

11. Strengthen and modernize our military, making it, without question, the strongest and most powerful in the world.

12. Keep the U.S. dollar as the world's reserve currency.

13. Fight for and protect Social Security and Medicare with no cuts, including no changes to the retirement age.

14. Cancel the electric vehicle mandate and cut costly and burdensome regulations.

15. Cut federal funding for any school pushing critical race theory, radical gender ideology, and other inappropriate racial, sexual, or political content on our children.

16. Keep men out of women's sports.

17. Deport pro-Hamas radicals and make our college campuses safe and patriotic again.

18. Secure our elections, including same-day voting, voter identification, paper ballots, and proof of citizenship.

19. Unite our country by bringing it to new and record levels of success.

CREATING A PUBLIC PLATFORM

Learning from the 2024 Presidential Campaign

Here we have the platform for the Democratic Party, focusing on the presidential platform. Each of the major parties also create platforms at the state level. Those state platforms will likely contain information on issues specific to a given state as well as issues that are national in scope. You should take time to research those platforms for the state you live in.

DEMOCRATIC PARTY STATEMENT:

"The Platform focuses on priorities for Democrats up and down the ballot, from growing the economy to lowering costs for families; tackling the climate crisis and securing energy independence; closing the racial wealth gap and investing in small businesses; restoring Roe v. Wade as the law of the land; protecting communities from the scourge of gun violence and protecting freedoms for all Americans; and securing our border and strengthening American leadership worldwide."

DEMOCRATIC PARTY 2024 PRESIDENTIAL PLATFORM

1. Cut middle-class taxes and eliminate taxes on tips.

2. Expand the Child Tax Credit and provide $6,000 for newborns.

3. Cap prices on groceries, rent, prescription drugs, and healthcare to combat inflation.

4. Build 3 million affordable homes and offer $25,000 in down payment assistance for first-time homebuyers.

5. Enact laws to curb corporate rent-gouging and speculative housing purchases.

6. Lower the cost of insulin and cap seniors' out-of-pocket Medicare expenses.

7. Codify the right to abortion and restore Roe v. Wade protections nationwide.

8. Invest in clean energy jobs while maintaining domestic energy independence.

9. Enforce environmental justice policies in underserved communities.

10. Strengthen voting rights protections and oppose voter suppression efforts.

11. Advance civil rights, including protections for LGBTQ+ individuals.

12. Reform immigration with increased border enforcement and a path to citizenship.

13. Increase funding for border technology and law enforcement.

14. Pass universal background checks and ban assault weapons.

15. Expand red-flag laws to keep guns out of dangerous hands.

16. Modernize the military while strengthening diplomatic alliances like NATO.

17. Continue U.S. support for Ukraine and de-escalation in the Middle East.

18. Cut federal funding to schools that teach racial or sexual content deemed inappropriate (while opposing book bans and censorship).

19. Cancel student debt for low-income borrowers and expand access to higher education.

20. Secure U.S. elections through transparency, paper ballot audits, and expanded access to voting.

Notes:

WHO IS YOUR TARGET AUDIENCE?

In order to craft a campaign message, you must know who your audience is. Who is likely to support you? Who is most likely to care about the issues you care about? What kinds of issues and messages typically appeal to your target audience? Knowing the answer to this question, and having identified the people to whom you can best appeal to support you or your cause — will allow you to develop your **campaign message**.

Three reasons why people would bother to vote for you/your cause?

Yes, having a famous name is important. Friends, family, and people who know you from school or church are more likely to vote for you. Having said this, the vast majority of people will want a certain question answered before they vote for you: They want to know why you have earned their vote. What have you said or done that _they believe_ earns you their support? The answer to this question will likely relate to one of the following three reasons:

1. They believe that your election will help **make their lives better**.

2. They believe that **you care** about what they care about.

3. They believe **you are qualified** to do something about the things you say you believe in, and will make their lives better.

KEY VALUES

What key value or values do you share with your audience?

As they say, "talk is cheap." A popular complaint about politicians is that they tend to make promises they can't keep. This raises the question, did they really believe in the issues they espoused, or did they just talk about those issues because they thought they could get people to vote for them? You can say all the right things, but not win because the voters didn't sense that you shared their values. In their hearts, they want to know that you identify with them.

List three key shared values.

1.
2.
3.

Linking Your Campaign Issues to a Shared Value with the Voters

Before you can create a campaign message, you must first lay a foundation of the issues you are running on and how these issues connect with one or all of the three reasons people would be willing to vote for you.

1. Make their lives better
2. You care
3. You are qualified

You are not running for President. You don't have to have a position on every issue being discussed in the national party platforms. Focusing on a handful of key issues that are important to you and the voters is a much better strategy. But, while listing issues to run on may sound simple, you must take care in how you choose them. There are many issues you may be asked about. Don't build your campaign around a series of "talking points?" Instead, build your campaign around a core set of issues that reflect key values and beliefs shared by you and your voters.

There are three levels that require your attention when choosing the issues you will build your campaign around. To illustrate these three levels, let's pick one of the issues in both the Democrat and Republican party platforms.

1. The first is what we'll call the **"issue level"** what are the specific facts of the issue? As an example, let's pick the issue: **lowering costs for families**. While different people may refer to this in different ways (i.e., inflation, the price of everything, why can't I afford a burger at McDonalds, etc.) they all relate to this idea that we need to lower costs for families.

2. **Idea level** — what are the philosophical whys and why not's of the issue? The way the Republican's phrased this issue was to refer to it this way: "End Inflation and Make America Affordable Again." In Chapter Four of their platform, the Republicans introduce their philosophical appeal this way:

    > Republicans offer a plan to make the American Dream affordable again. We commit to reducing Housing, Education, and Healthcare costs, while lowering everyday expenses, and increasing opportunities.

    In their platform, Democrats introduce their philosophical appeal this way on page 19 of their platform:

    > Today, our economy is growing, wages are rising, and a record number of Americans have good jobs. But for too many hard-working families, the cost of living is too high. Lowering costs is Democrats' number one economic priority.

    Please note that at the "idea level," voters will want to know what you **HAVE DONE** If you are the incumbent. If your rhetoric does not match your record, this will cause a problem for you. If you are a challenger, then you may not have a record of accomplishment you can point to. The question that potential voters should ask — and that you must be prepared to answer — is this: How can I **TRUST YOU** to do what you promise? We can't answer that question for you in this book. **YOU** must be prepared to answer it on your own.

3. **Value level** — does what you propose resonate with their deeply held values and beliefs? This is the most important level. All the others don't matter if you don't connect on this one. On the next page are two "value level" concepts that might affect how you, as an elected official, might go about "lowering costs for families".

Values connect with key beliefs. I want to spend extra time on this topic. To do that, I need to introduce two concepts from political science. One is called "negative liberty." It is defined as "freedom from constraints or the interference of others." The other is "positive liberty." It is defined as "the ability – and provision of basic necessities – to pursue one's goals." (Source: Morone, James A. and Rogan Kersh. By the People: Debating American Government. Brief Fourth Edition. Oxford University Press, copy right 2019.) Allow me to illustrate these concepts.

Negative Liberty. When we talk about negative liberty, we mean that there should be fewer government laws and regulations that form artificial barriers preventing you from succeeding in life or in business. Ronald Reagan talked about "getting government off our backs and out of our pockets." This implies that you believe that government should allow you to be free to succeed or fail based on your best efforts, and that you should be free to donate to the charities you support, not the ones the government tells you are more deserving than others. And so, in answer to the question, "do you need help from the government," your answer is "That's a **NEGATIVE**."

Positive Liberty. Generally speaking, it is the idea that the entire economic system of America is rigged against you. That no matter what you do, you will fail because others are endowed with certain privileges that are not available to you. And so, to "even the score", you need government assistance to enjoy the liberty our founding fathers talked about. To articulate this, Bill Clinton, Barack Obama, Bernie Sanders and others have said that "The rich should pay their fair share" – implying that some other group of people (not you) should pay more taxes and that other people (like you) should get more from the government. And so, in answer to the question, "do you need help from the government," your answer is you desire **POSITIVE** help so that you can exercise the liberties you would like to enjoy, but can't afford.

To examine this in the context of our example issue about **lowering costs for families,** here are the **"Value Level"** statements of the two political parties from their **2024** platforms:

Republicans

The Republican Party stands for a patriotic "America First" Economic Policy. ... We will prioritize Domestic Production, and ensure National Independence in essential goods and services. Together, **we will build a Strong, Self-reliant,** and Prosperous America. **(Emphasis added)**

Democrats

By **leveraging the benefits of federal grants** for infrastructure, manufacturing and services, we will seek to ensure that all Americans have the opportunity to participate in the American Dream. **(Emphasis added)**

And so, at the basic value level, the Republican Party is advocating self-reliance and "negative liberty" while the Democrat Part is advocating reliance on government grants of money and "positive liberty". The election will be decided based on which party can attract the most voters that supports its **value level** vision for America.

Different Values and key beliefs concerning the meaning of liberty

"Negative Liberty"

_____

_____

_____

"Positive Liberty"

_____

_____

_____

IDENTIFYING YOUR TARGET VOTERS

In our last section, we choose a topic which both political party platforms have taken a position on. What about YOUR campaign for office? Let's say that you have some issues that you feel you want to build a campaign message around. But now, we need to ask our **first question**: Which voters are the people who will likely respond to your message?

When Ronald Reagan ran for President, he set out to identify certain core issues that he wanted to focus on. He defined his number one problem of growing the economy this way. He said that "Government is the problem." Government stood in the way of making America prosperous again. He said he wanted to "get government off our backs and out of our pockets." Who was he likely speaking to? Who was his audience? Business owners who wanted to grow their businesses, or welfare recipients who wanted more benefits from the federal government? Clearly, it was the first group.

A **second question** that needs to be asked is this: Why should people believe that you can deliver on your promises — regardless of what your promises might be? In other words, are you a **CREDIBLE** person who can speak to that issue? In Ronald Reagan's case, he had been the Governor of California for eight years, from 1967 to 1975. California is the largest state in the country. So, in terms of credibility, if he could run the state of California, he was probably capable of running the United States of America.

Here is a **third question**. No matter how many issues may become factors in your upcoming election, whether you are running for the town's dog catcher or the governor of your state, you have to limit what you are going to talk about to only a handful of issues, and primarily, concentrate on only two or three. This will allow you to preserve your campaign's focus on the most important issues in your campaign. The question is, how do you zero in on these most important issues, and explain to the voters why how they are connected and why you are the best qualified candidate to solve these problems?

Remember, you'll want to stay on message, and avoid the temptation to go off chasing other side topics down a rabbit hole when, in fact, most voters really don't care about those other topics.

THE ISSUE BOX ASSIGNMENT

NAME THE POLITICAL OFFICE YOU ARE THINKING OF RUNNING FOR:
_____

Suppose you are considering ten issues. What are they?

List the ten issues that you feel relate to the political office you want to run for:

1.

2.

3.

4.

5.

6.

7.

8.

9.

10.

TOP THREE ISSUES

Now, to preserve your campaign's focus, you will need to concentrate on only three of these issues.

How should you decide which three? If you were really running a political campaign, you would at this point want to send out a survey to potential voters and ask them to tell you which issues are the most important. If you're reading this book, you're probably **NOT** running for political office in the near future. So, doing a professional survey is likely out of the question. However, you can still go to friends and family to just ask them to pick what **THEY** think are the top three issues out of the ten you listed.

Now that you have a list of ten issues, find at least ten different people to rank, **IN ORDER**, (1 through ten) what they think should be the top issues. Have them assign the number "10" to the number one issue and the number "1" to the least important issue.

Oh, and one last thing.

On a scale of **1** to **5** where **1** is "terrible" and **5** is "terrific", have them say how credible of a spokesperson you are on each of the ten issues. Please note: You might be a "5" on 2 issues, a "4" on 3 issues, a "3" on one issue, a "2" on four issues, and not be a "1" or "terrible" on any of the issues.

Once you have gotten all of the information back add up the score for each issue and the score for how credible a spokesperson you might be on that issue. Total the scores for these two rating criteria in the totals column.

EVALUATING ISSUES

Let's say that you have gone out and found ten issues and people ranked them **1** through ten, with **10** being most important and **1** being least. Also, they thought about your qualifications and experienced, and on a scale of **1** to **5**, with **1** meaning your qualifications and experience are "terrible" to deal with that issue, and a **5** meaning your qualifications and experience make you a "terrific" choice to deal with that issue, they've also rated your abilities on each of the ten issues.

Here are the results from our imaginary survey. The issues are listed from **A** to **J**: we're not using actual issues as we don't want to distract you from seeing how this is all put together.

Issues Rating Worksheet

Issues	Importance	Position	Total Score
A	1	4	5
B	10	1	11
C	9	5	14
D	8	2	10
E	3	2	5
F	7	5	12
G	5	3	8
H	4	1	5
I	2	3	5
J	6	4	10

With this example in mind, take the surveys you got back from the people you asked and construct a similar Issues Rating Worksheet. Don't go on to the next step in the assignment until you've done that.

Analyzing The Results of your Issues Rating Worksheet

Next, we want to take our ten issues and put them on a graph with four corners — or quadrants, as in the graph below. These quadrants are labeled as follows:
Q1 Very Important/Poor Position
Q2 Very Important/Good Position
Q3 Less Important/Poor Position
Q4: Less Important/Good Position

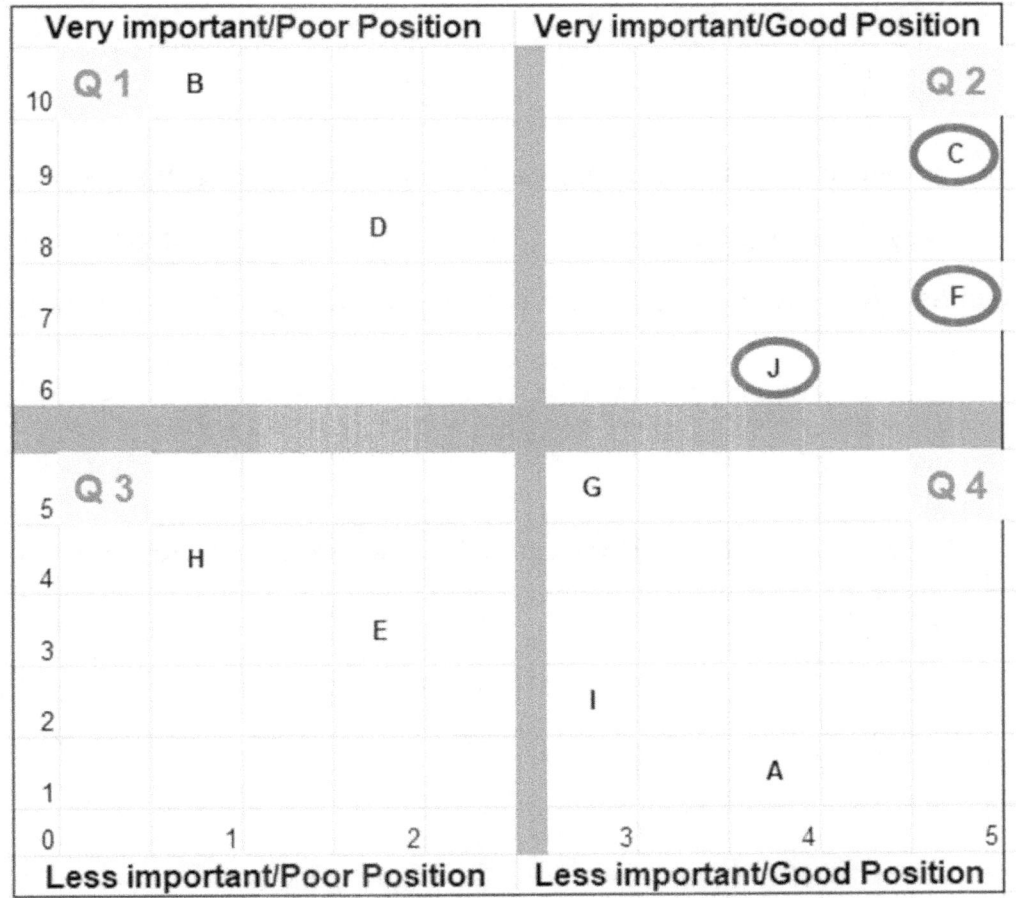

In Q1, issues B and D are very important to voters, but you're seen as weak on them—making you a less credible spokesperson there.

In Q3, issues E and H are not seen as important, and you're not viewed as strong on them either.

In Q4, issues A, G, and I are less important but ones where you're seen as effective.

Your top priority should be Q2—issues C, F, and J. These are highly important to voters, and you're already seen as a strong, credible voice. Focus your messaging here to align your strengths with voter priorities.

Should you develop position statements on the other issues? **Of course, you should!** Should you build campaign messages, slogans and commercials around those other issues? **No, you should not!** For example, if you focus on issues B and D in your campaign messaging, you risk having another candidate who is MORE credible than you steal the issue from you. Thus, every time you speak on topic B and D, you are bringing to the voters' attention the strengths of your opponent!

In conclusion, as we end this chapter, be sure to access the Issues Worksheet and Issues Survey Form we've provided. Once you have identified the key Campaign Issues, you will be ready to create your campaign vision and message.

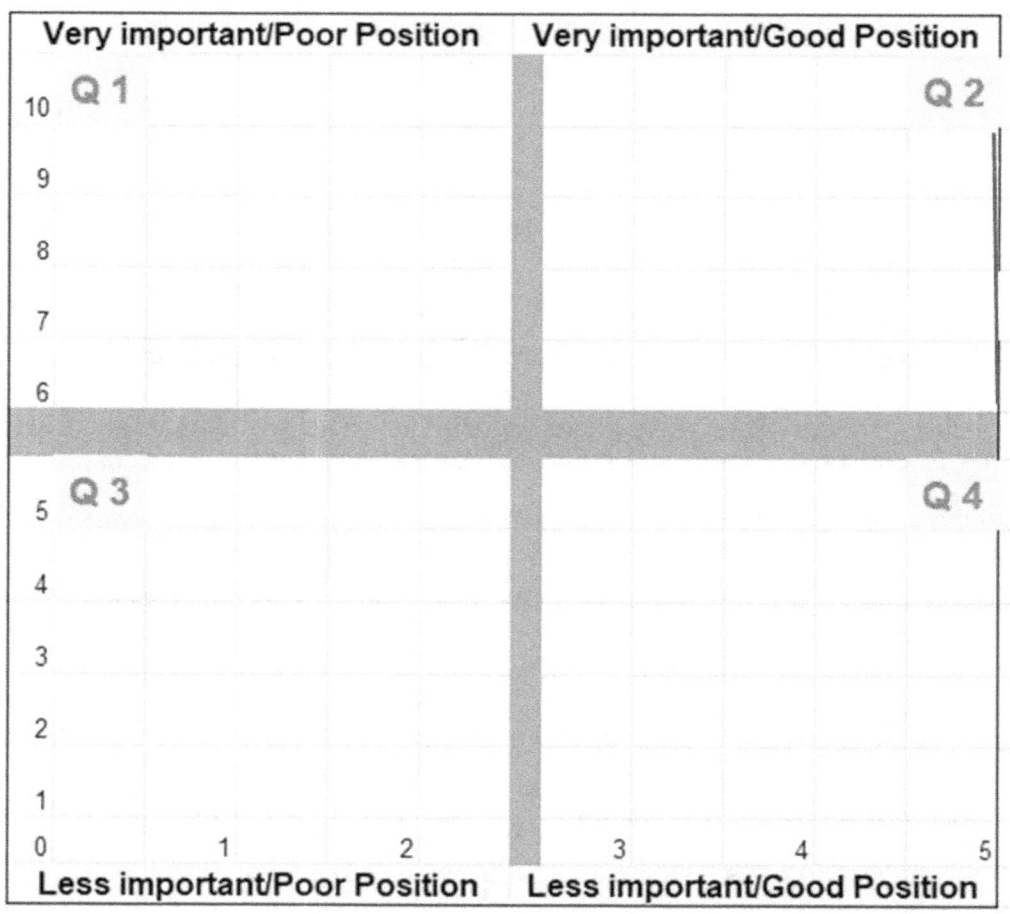

Issues Rating Worksheet			
Issues	Importance	Position	Total Score
A			
B			
C			
D			
E			
F			
G			
I			
J			
K			

Issues Rating Worksheet			
Issues	Importance	Position	Total Score
A			
B			
C			
D			
E			
F			
G			
I			
J			
K			

Issues Rating Worksheet			
Issues	Importance	Position	Total Score
A			
B			
C			
D			
E			
F			
G			
I			
J			
K			

Issues Rating Worksheet			
Issues	Importance	Position	Total Score
A			
B			
C			
D			
E			
F			
G			
I			
J			
K			

CHAPTER SEVEN

ALL ABOUT MESSAGING

Campaign Message Exercise, Complete your Campaign Message Box Assignment

DEVELOPING YOUR CAMPAIGN MESSAGE

In the last chapter, we talked about three levels of an issue. Let's briefly recap those three levels:

- **Issue level** — what are the specifics?
- **Idea level** — what are the philosophical whys and why not's of the issue?
- **Value level** — does what you propose resonate with their deeply held values and beliefs? This is the most important level. All the others don't matter if you don't connect on this one.

In this chapter, we will dig into this third level, the value level in order to develop your **campaign message**. A campaign message is **NOT** your list of proposals of what you will do if elected. It's also not a simple catch phrase or slogan. Keep in mind that people are constantly bombarded with information. You don't waste their time and attention when you have it.

That is why your message must be simple, to the point, and repeated often. It should say why you are running, and why people should vote for you or your cause. Again, let's return to a review of some of the things Ronald Reagan did.

President Reagan ran on such issues as lower taxes, a strong national defense, less government regulation and personal freedom grounded in moral living. But his campaign message was much more than the sum of his issues. **He used rhetoric that painted a picture of a better future, such as saying that** America is a "shining city on a hill," and that it was "morning in America." He talked about how you and I should decide how to spend our money instead of the government spending it "for" us.

Think back to chapters one and two, where we spent time looking at the experiences and personal backgrounds of various elected office holders, particularly how we looked at the experiences that shaped leaders like Davy Crockett and Abraham Lincoln. For people to believe in you as a credible candidate, your past experiences and who you are must demonstrate that you live what you say — that you walk the talk. It is out of your past experiences that you will develop a vision for what you think should be done. Your vision must connect with voters' values which helps them identify with you and want to vote for you.

List experience and accomplishments, stories, examples and facts that you could share about yourself.

_____
_____
_____
_____
_____
_____
_____
_____
_____
_____
_____
_____
_____
_____
_____
_____
_____

CREATING YOUR CAMPAIGN MESSAGE

It's time for you to start thinking about an elective position you might run for. Let's begin by think about how to write a campaign message that you can use in any circumstance. Such a message is sometimes called an "elevator speech." The idea is that if you are speaking with someone in an elevator, you should be able to say it between the time you and someone else gets on an elevator and the time one of you gets off. Here are seven characteristics of a good campaign message:

1. It must be short.

2. It must be truthful & credible.

3. It must be persuasive and important to voters.

4. It must show a contrast between you and your opponent.

5. It must speak from the heart.

6. It must be targeted to your audience.

7. It must be repeated again and again.

With these seven characteristics in mind, complete the following assignment.

- Look at the **Issue Box Analysis** you completed in **Chapter 6**. Using that information as a starting point, make a list of all the reasons why voters should vote for you and your party.

- Choose the most compelling reasons from the above list and write a brief statement about your candidacy. In this statement, answer two questions:

    * Why are you running for this office? Your answer should reveal what you are most passionate about.
    * Why should someone vote for you? How you answer this reveals your vision for the future.

- Read the statement aloud and time yourself. Edit it down until it takes less than a minute to say.

- If you go over a minute, you must continue to trim your message. Remove any long phrases or explanations. Remember that voters will not be paying attention to a long speech. Besides, they are going to get off the elevator any second and leave you behind.

REFINING YOUR CAMPAIGN MESSAGE EXERCISE

- Grade your message against the seven characteristics of a good message.

    For example:
    * Is it credible and truthful?
    * Do you backup your statements with personal experience from your past?
    * Are you talking about things that are important to your target voters?
    * Do you offer a clear choice between your candidate and your major opponents?
- Now rewrite your statement, including those things you missed the first time. Keep it under a minute.
- Memorize it.
- **Go and repeat it to several friends.** Ask them to give you honest feedback.
- After considering the feedback from your friends, write your fully refined Campaign Message on the next page.

DRAW A COMIC STRIP OF YOU ON AN ELEVATOR, MEETING A STRANGER, AND HAVE FUN GIVING YOUR ONE MINUTE CAMPAIGN MESSAGE

SHARE YOUR TOP TIPS FOR EACH PLATFORM:

FACEBOOK:

X / TWITTER

IN PERSON COMMUNICATION:

INSTAGRAM:

TRADITIONAL MEDIA:

TEN TIPS FOR OPTIMIZING SOCIAL MEDIA

1. Define Your Message Clearly.

Before posting, know what you stand for. Create 2–3 core messages (e.g., transparency, local jobs, parental rights) and stick to them. Consistency builds trust and recognition.

2. Be Authentic & Personable.

People vote for people, not just policies. Post behind-the-scenes moments, family life, or real-time reflections. Voters connect with candidates who feel human, not scripted.

3. Use Video Strategically.

Short, direct-to-camera videos build trust fast. Use Instagram Reels, TikTok, YouTube Shorts, and Facebook to explain positions, share personal stories, or respond to current events.

4. Engage With Comments & Messages.

Responding to voters' comments or questions builds community and trust. Even a "thanks for your thoughts" goes a long way. Prioritize real engagement over canned replies.

5. Post Consistently, Not Constantly.

A steady rhythm matters more than frequency. Aim for 3–5 quality posts per week on key platforms, rather than flooding your feed with filler.

6. Use Platform-Specific Strengths.

Facebook for local events, family-focused messages, and fundraising.

Instagram for visuals, quotes, and personal moments.

Twitter/X for quick reactions and news commentary.

TikTok for short, bold messaging and reaching younger audiences.

YouTube for campaign trailers, long-form interviews, and speeches.

7. Use Hashtags & Geo-Tags.

Target your audience by using local hashtags, district names, or relevant movements (e.g., #HoosiersForChange or #IN3Votes). Geo-tag events to connect with locals.

8. Amplify Supporters' Content.

Repost or share your followers' endorsements, event photos, or videos. It shows momentum and encourages others to share too.

9. Stay Positive—but Be Bold.

Avoid personal attacks. Instead, take strong stands on key issues and contrast your ideas with opponents' positions respectfully and powerfully.

10. Track Analytics & Adapt.

Use insights (on Facebook, Instagram, etc.) to see what works. Watch for what gets likes, shares, and saves—and do more of it. Drop what doesn't

CONSTRUCTING YOUR MESSAGE BOX

Hopefully, you'll have opportunities to speak longer than the time it takes to travel in an elevator! Remember those speeches you worked on back in **Chapter 4**? You will want to turn your campaign message into an expanded campaign speech — a speech that is often referred to as "The Stump Speech." We'll come back to your **Stump Speech** at the end of this chapter.

On a large piece of paper, draw the following table. Download the "Message Box" document and write out what you think people who agree/disagree with you say about you/say about themselves. If you can understand these points of view, you can shape your message in such a way to communicate your campaign vision.

1. **WHAT WE SAY ABOUT US**
    Include the positive elements you identified in the Campaign Message Exercise.
2. **WHAT WE SAY ABOUT THEM**
    What do you wish voters knew about our opponent and their stand on the issues so that people wouldn't vote for them?
3. **WHAT THEY SAY ABOUT US**
    Why, from your opponents' point of view, should people NOT vote for you?
4. **WHAT THEY SAY ABOUT THEMSELVES**
    Why, from your opponents' point of view, should people vote for them and not you?

What we say about us:	What they say about us:
What we say about them:	**What they say about themselves:**

If done correctly, this **MESSAGE BOX** should outline everything that could possibly be said during the campaign. It will help prepare you for the attacks you **KNOW** will come. And, you will be prepared to emphasize the positive parts of your campaign message, while bringing to the voters' attention the failings of your opponent's position/experience/values.

THE STUMP SPEECH ASSIGNMENT

Back in Chapter 4, you created and practiced delivering **The Persuasive Speech**. Take the concept for that speech and rework it now into your "stump speech". A stump speech is a standardized campaign speech that expands on your campaign message whenever you speak before a new audience. Again, plan on it being **5 to 7 minutes long**. Here are some video examples to help you think about how to create a stump speech. As before,

1. First, outline the speech.
2. Incorporate your campaign message.
3. Provide examples, in story form, to illustrate key ideas.
4. Talk about how you are different from your opponent.
5. Take humors jabs at your opponent.
6. Explain what your vision is, and what you will do if elected.
7. Practice it, and then deliver to an audience.

Here are some short videos
about what a stump speech is and some examples:

What is a Stump Speech?
https://youtu.be/SsaQsJeZSIw?si=wl2n17-EvPQ7GM7y

Barack Obama 2004 Democratic Keynote Speech:
https://youtu.be/OFPwDe22CoY?si=hnwLca-oNmK4kUMp

Ronald Reagan: A Time for Choosing, 1964.
https://youtu.be/N0w_eaUVthM?si=I62MVcP5qzimggFX

Pop-Up Politics: Newt Gingrich's Iowa Stump Speech
https://youtu.be/Gp47Q28ts9I?si=rLpuoWGs1X1MwP_3

STUMP SPEECH OUTLINE

CHAPTER EIGHT

ALL ABOUT BUILDING YOUR NETWORK

— Stakeholder Identification Assignment

BUILDING A CAMPAIGN COALITION

Up until now, we've been talking about the things you might do as a volunteer in a political campaign, or preparing yourself to become a candidate for office. It's interesting to think about famous people of the past, and how they overcame obstacles by persevering to achieve a vision they believed in. But then there's the actual process of running for office. One of the things that every candidate running for public offices learns is that there are interest groups who might be potential allies. They may offer to have you, or the candidate you're volunteering for, come speak to their supporters. Or, they may sponsor a candidate forum and invite you as one of the candidates to come give your stump speech, and to answer questions from the audience. They may even want to sponsor a debate between you and one or more of your opponents.

Or consider the fact that there are interest groups and voting blocks out there whom you would like to "court" so you can win their support. You might author an opinion piece/blog post where you stake out your position on a topic they care about. Before writing it, you might find out which interest groups already exist that support the same things you support, and target publication of your article or YouTube video specifically to that audience.

In this chapter, we'll think about identifying and courting interest groups and organizations who might be logical allies in your political campaign. You want to build a coalition of groups who will help you get your campaign message out to everyday voters. Remember, these interest groups already have audiences that listen to their leaders on a regular basis. They have their own social media groups that might be eager to read about your position on an issue they care about/watch a short video where you lay out your position on the issues they care about most.

Identify Stakeholders Who Might Be Potential Supporters of Your Congressional Candidate

"Stakeholders" are individuals or groups with a vested interest or concern in something, especially a business or a political issue. Brainstorm about a list of stakeholders who might have an interest in your Congressional candidate, who they might be, and why they would either support or oppose your candidate. To get you started, here is a list at least 5 categories of stakeholders that a political campaign needs to identify and build relationships with.

1. Identify stakeholders in the following business categories:
    a. Business groups (such as Rotary clubs, Chambers of Commerce, etc.)
    b. Prominent business owners.
    c. Trade Associations.

2. Identify stakeholders in the following religious categories:
    a. Ministerial groups (not just Christian, but other faiths as well)
    b. Key places of worship.
    c. Key not-for-profit/para-ministry groups (such as faith based homeless shelters of food pantries.)

3. Political party organizations:
    a. Republican/Democrat/Libertarian clubs.
    b. County/township political leaders and key officials.
    c. Police/Fire/Teacher groups.

4. Local politically active interest groups:
    a. Conservative groups like Moms for liberty/Tea Party/similar groups.
    b. Liberal groups like Black Lives Matter, LGBTQ/similar groups.
    c. Not-for-profit 501-c3 and c4 groups that align with, or oppose your beliefs.
    d. Veterans Organizations.

5. Local media outlets:
    a. Newspapers.
    b. Radio stations.
    c. Podcasts.
    d. Social media groups.
    e. Bloggers.

STAKEHOLDER IDENTIFICATION ASSIGNMENT:

On each of the next five pages you will:

1. Find one group/organization/institution from each of the 5 categories Listed on the previous page.

2. Identify the following information for each:
   Name and contact information for the head person.

3. Their webpage and/or social media page(s).

4. Provide a brief explanation of what they support/do/believe in.
   Typically, most social media pages will have some sort of "About Us" page where you can read and find this information.

5. Write a one to three sentence explanation of why your candidate should meet with this stakeholder organization and talk about their campaign.

BUSINESSES

I chose this group, prominent business owner, or trade association:

a. Name and Contact information for the head person.
_____
_____
_____

b. Their webpage and/or social media page(s).
_____
_____
_____

c. A brief explanation of what they support/do/believe in. Typically, most social media pages will have some sort of "About Us" page where you can read and find this information.
_____
_____
_____

d. A one to three-sentence explanation of why your candidate should meet with this Stakeholder organization and talk about their campaign.
_____
_____
_____
_____
_____
_____
_____

RELIGIOUS GROUPS

I chose this religious group, place of worship, or not-for-profit:.

a. Name and Contact information for the head person.
_____
_____
_____

b. Their webpage and/or social media page(s).
_____
_____
_____

c. A brief explanation of what they support/do/believe in. Typically, most social media pages will have some sort of "About Us" page where you can read and find this information.
_____
_____
_____

d. A one to three-sentence explanation of why your candidate should meet with this Stakeholder organization and talk about their campaign.
_____
_____
_____
_____
_____
_____
_____

POLITICAL PARTY ORGANIZATIONS

I chose this political party organization:

a. Name and Contact information for the head person.
_____
_____
_____

b. Their webpage and/or social media page(s).
_____
_____
_____

c. A brief explanation of what they support/do/believe in. Typically, most social media pages will have some sort of "About Us" page where you can read and find this information.
_____
_____
_____

d. A one to three-sentence explanation of why your candidate should meet with this Stakeholder organization and talk about their campaign.
_____
_____
_____
_____
_____
_____
_____

POLITICALLY ACTIVE INTEREST GROUP

I chose this group:

a. Name and Contact information for the head person.
_____
_____
_____

b. Their webpage and/or social media page(s).
_____
_____
_____

c. A brief explanation of what they support/do/believe in. Typically, most social media pages will have some sort of "About Us" page where you can read and find this information.
_____
_____
_____

d. A one to three-sentence explanation of why your candidate should meet with this Stakeholder organization and talk about their campaign.
_____
_____
_____
_____
_____
_____
_____
_____

LOCAL MEDIA OUTLETS

I chose this local media outlet:

a. **N**ame and **C**ontact information for the head person.
_____
_____
_____

b. Their webpage and/or social media page(s).
_____
_____
_____

c. A brief explanation of what they support/do/believe in. Typically, most social media pages will have some sort of "About Us" page where you can read and find this information.
_____
_____
_____

d. A one to three-sentence explanation of why your candidate should meet with this **S**takeholder organization and talk about their campaign.
_____
_____
_____
_____
_____
_____
_____

CHAPTER NINE

YOUR CAPSTONE PROJECT!

Congratulations!

You are the Campaign Coordinator for your Congressional Candidate

YOUR CAPSTONE PROJECT

Throughout this book, you have completed various assignments.

Here is a recap of all you have done:

Chapter One: A 150 word introduction of yourself specifying your qualifications.

Chapter Two: Researched a Congressional Candidate, Identified Qualities Possessed by a Political Leader.

Chapter Three: Completed Biographical Sketches of Davy Crockett and Abraham Lincoln, Identified Qualities that Made Davy Crockett and Abraham Lincoln Great Leaders.

Chapter Four: Analyzed Twelve Typical Campaign Volunteer Tasks, Compared & Contrasted the Types of skills / Personal Characteristics Needed to do these tasks.

Chapter Five: Prepared and Delivered Three Types of Speeches, and received evaluations and constructive criticism from an audience of your peers.

Chapter Six: Completed the Issues Box Assignment, Completed the Issues Rating Worksheet Assignment.

Chapter Seven: Completed the Campaign Message Exercise, Completed your Campaign Message Box Assignment.

Chapter Eight: Completed your Stakeholder Identification Assignment.

Now, you are ready for your Capstone Project!

CONGRATULATIONS!

You are the Campaign Coordinator for your Congressional Candidate

Let's imagine that you have now been appointed the Campaign Coordinator for your Congressional Candidate. You can't do everything by yourself. You will want to hire a few key campaign staff people. Their job will to be to recruit volunteers to help them do all the things they have to do. You need to take what you have learned and create a plan to run the campaign. You need to start by hiring key campaign staff people to fill the following 7 campaign positions:

1. County Coordinator.

2. Volunteer Recruitment Coordinator and Committee.

3. County Canvass Coordinator and Committee.

4. Fund Raising/Event Coordinator and Committee.

5. Organization Coordinator & Committee.

6. Precinct Captain Coordinator & Committee.

7. Communications Coordinator & Committee.

To fill each position, pick someone you know from your circle of friends, family, teachers and acquaintances. For each "hire," write a paragraph that explains what it is they will be doing in this position, and why you chose them.

Identify the key issues for this campaign. What are they, and why? Create your Campaign Message and draft a Stump Speech for your candidate. Also, look at the geographic boundaries of this congressional district. What are the different stakeholder groups you will need to build a campaign coalition with? **Provide maps**, lists, graphs and charts, as well as a written report that lays out your plans to get your Congressional Candidate elected.

BUILD YOUR TEAM

To fill each position, pick someone you know from your circle of friends, family, teachers and acquaintances. For each "hire," write a paragraph that explains what it is they will be doing in this position, and why you chose them.

1. County Coordinator.
2. Volunteer Recruitment Coordinator and Committee.
3. County Canvass Coordinator and Committee.
4. Fund Raising/Event Coordinator and Committee.
5. Organization Coordinator & Committee.
6. Precinct Captain Coordinator & Committee.
7. Communications Coordinator & Committee.

1. COUNTY COORDINATOR CHOICE:

_____
_____
_____
_____
_____
_____
_____
_____
_____
_____
_____
_____

2. VOLUNTEER RECRUITMENT COORDINATOR AND COMMITTEE:

3. COUNTY CANVASS COORDINATOR AND COMMITTEE:

4 FUND RAISING/EVENT COORDINATOR AND COMMITTEE:

_____
_____
_____
_____
_____
_____
_____
_____
_____
_____
_____
_____

5. ORGANIZATION COORDINATOR AND COMMITTEE:

_____
_____
_____
_____
_____
_____
_____
_____
_____
_____
_____
_____

6. PRECINCT CAPTAIN COORDINATOR AND COMMITTEE:

7. COMMUNICATIONS COORDINATOR AND COMMITTEE:

IDENTIFY THE KEY ISSUES FOR THIS CAMPAIGN.

What are they, and why? Create your Campaign Message and draft a Stump Speech for your candidate to give. Also, look at the geographic boundaries of this congressional district. What are the different stakeholder groups you will need to build a campaign coalition with?

What are the key issues?

_____
_____
_____
_____
_____
_____
_____
_____
_____
_____
_____
_____

WHY ARE THESE ISSUES SO IMPORTANT?

_____
_____
_____
_____
_____
_____
_____
_____
_____
_____
_____
_____
_____
_____
_____
_____
_____
_____
_____
_____
_____
_____
_____

TALK OF THE TOWN

Imagine listening to what is being said
about your candidate and the opponents.

Whose is saying what? How can you shape the narrative?
Use the two following pages to refine your insights.

What we say about us:

What we say about them:

What they say about us:

What they say about themselves:

CONSIDERING THE KEY ISSUES, CREATE YOUR CAMPAIGN MESSAGE.

PROVIDE A MAP HERE THAT SHOWS THE BOUNDARIES OF THIS CONGRESSIONAL DISTRICT.

DRAFT A STUMP SPEECH FOR YOUR CANDIDATE.

Notes:

OUTLINE.

NOTES, LISTS, GRAPHS, CHARTS, AND MAPS THAT WILL BE HELPFUL IN THIS CAMPAIGN.

CREATE A LIST OF 10 THINGS YOU SHOULD NEVER DO DURING AN ELECTION:

DRAW A CARTOON ABOUT A CANDIDATE AND CAMPAIGN TEAM WHO DID ALL TEN OF THOSE THINGS:

CREATE A LIST OF 10 THINGS YOU SHOULD DEFINITELY DO DURING AN ELECTION:

DRAW A CARTOON ABOUT A CANDIDATE AND CAMPAIGN TEAM WHO DID ALL TEN OF THOSE THINGS:

PROVIDE A WRITTEN REPORT THAT LAYS OUT YOUR PLANS TO HELP GET YOUR CANDIDATE ELECTED.

LIST TEN IDEAS FOR USING SOCIAL MEDIA AND YOUTUBE TO PROMOTE YOUR CANDIDATE.

CHAPTER TEN

RUN
WIN
LEAD

Communicating your vision,
developing your voice, leading with honor.

WRITE A NEW 150 BIOGRAPHY!
COMPARE IT TO THE ONE AT THE BEGINNING.

WRITE A BLOG POST ANNOUNCING YOUR INTENTION TO RUN FOR OFFICE:

RUN! WHY SHOULD YOU RUN FOR OFFICE? WRITE A LETTER TO POTENTIAL SUPPORTERS:

RUN! WHY ARE YOU THE BEST LEADER? COMPARE YOURSELF TO THE IMAGINARY OPPONENT.

_____
_____
_____
_____
_____
_____
_____
_____
_____
_____
_____
_____
_____
_____
_____
_____
_____
_____
_____

YOU WIN!
YOUR SPEECH FOR WINNING AN ELECTION:

YOU LOSE!
YOUR SPEECH FOR CONCEDING AN ELECTION:

LEAD! DAY ONE!
GOALS FOR YOUR FIRST 100 DAYS IN OFFICE:

LEAD! IT'S BEEN A YEAR!
YOUR STATE OF THE UNION/STATE/TOWN ADDRESS:

LEAD! A TRAGEDY HITS YOUR COMMUNITY! WRITE A SPEECH TO RESTORE HOPE AND ORDER:

LEAD! YOUR CONSTITUENTS WANT LOWER TAXES! EXPLAIN HOW YOU WILL CUT SPENDING:

LEAD! YOU CONTINUANTS WANT BETTER SERVICES! CREATE A PLAN TO PRIORITIZE SPENDING:

LEAD! YOUR CONSTITUENTS WANT MORE LIBERTY! EXPLAIN HOW YOU WILL FIGHT FOR THEIR RIGHTS:

_____
_____
_____
_____
_____
_____
_____
_____
_____
_____
_____
_____
_____
_____
_____
_____
_____

LEAD! YOUR PARTY DISAGREES WITH YOUR SPENDING CUTS, DEFEND THEM IN AN OPEN LETTER:

LEAD! YOUR STAFF HAS BEEN WORKING HARD. MORAL IS LOW. HOW WILL YOU ENCOURAGE THEM?

LEAD! YOU NEED BIPARTISIN SUPPORT TO ENACT ONE OF YOUR CAMPAIN PROMISES. WRITE A SPEECH:

LEAD! IT'S THE FOURTH OF JULY!
WRITE A SPEECH TO HONOR THE COST OF FREEDOM:

RUN WIN LEAD

Copyright © 2025

Standard License
This book is licensed for:
Personal and family use
Reproducible use with up to five students
in co-ops, micro-schools, or private tutoring

For classroom use with more than five students,
a school license is required.
Published by:
The Thinking Tree , LLC

Phone: 317.622.8852
Email: Contact@FunSchooling.com

Website: FunSchooling.com

www.ingramcontent.com/pod-product-compliance
Lightning Source LLC
Chambersburg PA
CBHW060232240426
43671CB00016B/2922